TALES
FROM THE
FRAUD
SQUAD

Willie McGee first made national headlines in 1967, scoring four goals in an All-Ireland under-21 football final win for Mayo. He went on to play for the Mayo senior team for many years; he was awarded the Garda Sports award in 2014, and the *Western People* Hall of Fame award in 2017. Well-known both inside and outside An Garda Síochána for his involvement in fraud investigation, McGee was then recruited by AXA Insurance to help set up a special investigation unit in their fight against fraud in their industry, the first of its kind in Ireland.

for the people and of the people. It was a privilege to protect and serve. The old uniform is still hanging in my wardrobe and there it will remain.

ACKNOWLEDGEMENTS

I would like to acknowledge the support and advice I have received from my family, especially my wife Elizabeth, while enduring the not-too-easy task of putting this book together. I'm also thankful to my friends who encouraged me to continue with the writing despite having to overcome the hardship of my stroke over six years ago.

I also appreciate the excellent support and encouragement I received from the team at Merrion Press. My thanks to Conor Graham, Maeve Convery, Wendy Logue, Sarah Doyle and to Patrick O'Donoghue, the commissioning editor who remained stoic with me throughout the editing of *Tales from the Fraud Squad*.

TALES
FROM THE
FRAUD
SQUAD

WILLIE McGEE

MERRION
PRESS

First published in 2022 by
Merrion Press
10 George's Street
Newbridge
Co. Kildare
www.merrionpress.ie

© Willie McGee, 2022

978 1 78537 359 6 (Paper)
978 1 78537 300 8 (Ebook)

A CIP catalogue record for this book is
available from the British Library.

Typeset in Sabon LT Std 11.5/17

Cover design by Fiachra McCarthy

Merrion Press is a member of Publishing Ireland

CONTENTS

AUTHOR'S NOTE

'There is a book in everyone,' she said to her listening audience. I was driving along as the woman on the radio described the book she had written about herself, adding that she had never done anything exciting in her life. When I got home, I grabbed my laptop and enumerated a long list of stories I could write about, covering my footballing days and my life in the Garda Síochána. I have regaled my family and friends over the years with these same stories and the advice has always been to get them all together in a book. *Tales from the Fraud Squad* is the result and I hope you will enjoy the grand variety of anecdotes that follows.

1

A NEWPORT CHILDHOOD

I don't know if there was a lot going on in the wider world on 15 May 1947, but there was a lot going on in mine because it was the day I was born. I was the fifth child of Kathleen and Charlie, two more were to follow.

In later years I found out that there'd been one major event earlier that winter – the unmerciful cold that had gripped the country for months. It was the Year of the Big Snow. My mother would have been pregnant during that frightful season of Arctic weather. I was told that the river in Newport was frozen solid for weeks on end and people went skating on it for fun. Every house got through a lot of turf that winter to keep the home fires burning.

My father was a postman and I'd say it was fairly testing trying to navigate the roads on your bicycle in those conditions. The same man could turn his hand to a lot of things. He was also a part-time insurance agent and factory clerk. He was a hunter, a fisherman, a gardener, a builder, a handyman, a sportsman and a volunteer in the community.

My mother was an O'Malley, the youngest of thirteen children born on Inishcuttle, one of the 365 islands in Clew Bay. She had the most wonderful singing voice. The island is tiny, about 800 metres in width and 250 metres north to south. It is close to the mainland and, like many islands up and down the west coast, its population dwindled down to just a few remaining families. The O'Malleys moved off it and set up home beside it in the parish of Kilmeena, between Westport and Newport. Eleven of the siblings emigrated. In fact, my mother never met her older brother Austin, because he had already left for Chicago by the time she was born and he never came home. I actually met him in Chicago in 1970, not long before he died. While I was there, he wanted to record a voice message that I could bring home to the sister he never met. He spoke into a reel-to-reel recorder. I brought the tape home and played it to my mother. We didn't have a phone at home so it was the first time she'd ever heard his voice. She got very emotional. At one point he says, 'My voice is cracked. I'm getting old.' After, he sang the first verse of 'When Irish Eyes are Smiling'. Those are the only words I can remember. It really upset my mother to hear them.

O'Malley, of course, is a famous Mayo surname. McGee isn't. My grandfather, Peter Paul McGee, was from Aughnacloy in Tyrone. He was a great horseman and fiddle player. He had come to Mayo some time in the early 1900s to work as a groomsman and farrier on the Newport House estate that had been owned by the O'Donel family for over a hundred years. Like many of the great landed estates across Ireland, the O'Donel estate and others owned by the Anglo-Irish gentry in Mayo were eventually broken up as a result of various Land Acts in the late 1800s and early 1900s, and divided among local farmers.

Newport House, in time, became a very fancy hotel where all sorts of VIPs and wealthy people would come to stay. My five sisters all worked in the hotel during their summer holidays. The Hollywood star Grace Kelly, Princess Grace of Monaco, stayed there a number of times. We claimed Princess Grace as one of our own; her grandfather, John Kelly, was born and raised in Drumulra, where the ruins of his ancestral home can be found about two miles outside Newport off the Castlebar Road. John was amongst the millions who departed these shores in the decades following the Great Famine in the 1840s.

One day, when Princess Grace was visiting in 1961, a gang of us teenagers and children went running after her car as it headed out the Castlebar Road. In fact, there were a couple of cars in her entourage. It was unbelievably exciting to have this famous star of the silver screen in our village. I was fourteen at the time. I was already a good runner so I was able to keep up with the cavalcade for a good few minutes. And lo and behold, didn't the princess roll down her window and compliment me on my curly red hair and lovely freckles! She had this big beaming smile and was incredibly glamorous. I was bowled over! I was delighted with myself; I felt like Gary Cooper and James Stewart rolled into one. You didn't have glamour like that in Newport every day, let me tell you.

Peter McGee married a local primary school teacher,

Brigid Hoban, and they had seven children. Uncle Harry was the only one of them who emigrated; he went to London. Charlie was born in 1914 and worked on the buildings in England in his twenties before moving home. My mother had also worked in England as a young woman. My father built the house on Melcomb Road that we grew up in, a fine two-storey house about half a mile from the harbour. The post office in the village serviced a wide rural area around it; there were seven postmen working out of it. Dad would be gone early in the morning doing his deliveries on his bicycle; eventually he got a wee motorbike, a Honda 50 I think, and finally a little car, a Mini. He'd get home in the afternoon and some days then he'd have to do his insurance rounds, collecting instalment payments from people around the town and countryside.

Built on the shore of Clew Bay, there was naturally a strong maritime influence on Newport. It had a seaweed factory on the quay that was owned by Bertie Staunton and then his son Myles, who would go on to become a Fine Gael TD and senator. Dad would do a regular couple of hours there weighing the seaweed – 'wrack' we called it – that was brought in by the local harvesters. It'd be put on a scales and weighed. The wrack would be processed into fertiliser, animal meal and an ingredient for cosmetics; hundreds of tons of it would be shipped out on big boats a couple of times a year. If a harvester landed in with a couple of tons of it, Dad would have to check to see there were no stones hiding in it to augment the weight. The Stauntons trusted that he'd do everything by the book because he was a straight-down-the-line man.

He kept a great garden, too, for spuds and all the kitchen vegetables. And when the hunting season kicked off, he was out with the gun and his red setter shooting pheasant and duck and woodcock and the like. The hills behind the house were crawling with rabbits and their beautiful white meat was often on our dinner plate. He'd have us out the back of the house holding the legs of the rabbits while he skinned them. The ducks and pheasants were plucked and roasted. There'd be fur and feathers flying. He kept a boat for fishing in the bay and for pulling in lobster and crab. We'd sell the lobster and crab to the Newport House Hotel. We picked shellfish out of the rock pools and sold it to a company in Kilmeena that exported it. Your hands would be blue with cold from the water.

In my teenage years I developed another way of making a few bob, through the use of my father's shotgun. A reward of a half crown (two and sixpence) was paid to anyone who could prove they had killed certain species of birds which were a danger to young fish either in the sea or the river. Cormorants (we called them black hags) and herons (we called them cranes) were the most culpable and the proof required was to produce their head to the Local Fisheries Board outside Newport. The head of the Board, excuse the pun, was a man called Jack Chambers, whose grandson and namesake is now a TD and the current Minister of State for Gaeltacht Affairs and Sport. The cartridge in each case would have cost my father six pence, but he didn't mind me creaming off the profit for good work done in saving and allowing young fish to develop.

As if he wasn't busy enough, Daddy also started a

handball club in the town and was its secretary for many years. He drove the project to build a 60x30 alley. It's derelict now, but there's a plaque in his honour on the wall, dedicated 'to the memory of Charlie McGee for his life-long contribution to the development of handball in Newport, 1938–1980.' My brother Peter inherited his love of the sport and became a top-class player on the national circuit, winning eighteen senior All-Ireland medals. He was in the *Guinness Book of Records* at one time for holding the greatest number of senior All-Ireland titles. Eventually he was overtaken by the late great Ducksie Walsh.

Dad would be gone most weekends to handball matches and although it was his first love, he was mad about Gaelic football too and played county for Mayo at junior level, winning two Connacht titles. His politics were Fianna Fáil; he was a Dev man, an *Irish Press* man. In fact, he bought the paper every single day, which was unusual in those times. Of an evening when he had all his work done, he'd read the paper and do the crossword. He'd play a few hands of cards with us too, but at some stage there was one more duty to be fulfilled – the rosary. Everyone had to get down on their knees to say the rosary. More often than not we'd be teasing the cat with the rosary beads instead of counting our Hail Marys.

From early morning to late in the evening Dad was at

his work in one way or another. It was all about providing for his wife and seven children. He'd always have the fire down before he left in the morning. That was his first job of the day. And last thing at night, he'd heap the ashes on the coals to keep it smouldering overnight so he could stoke it into life the next morning. Then he'd be gone and our mother would take over the running of the house. She cooked and baked and washed all day long and would sing a song as good as anyone you'd hear on the wireless. Like her husband, she was hard-working and honest and straightforward. She looked after us all, made sure we weren't in need of anything and was always on the ball relative to any colds or flus we might encounter. There were plenty of doses of 'black cows milk', a mixture of milk and porter (presumably Guinness), which only came in half-pint glass bottles and was a scarce enough commodity in those days. That was our homemade vitamins all wrapped up in one.

That was the world we grew up in, Charlie and Kathleen and their brood: Mary the eldest, followed by Peter, Teresa, Angela, myself, Kathleen and last but not least, Agnes, who arrived seven years after Kathleen. Granny O'Malley lived with us too until a ripe old age.

It was a wholesome, innocent childhood on the west coast of Ireland in the 1950s and '60s. We had warmth and security. There was work and there was play. We were fed the best of good rough food from the garden, the land and the sea. We were surrounded by the natural world; it was all on our doorstep: the hills and fields and woods and bogs, the Atlantic Ocean, the four seasons. You had

the Black Oak River flowing into the sea, spanned by the great railway viaduct that once upon a time carried trains on their way to Achill. The viaduct has seven arches and even though the trains stopped coming a long time ago, it remains, to this day, a mightily impressive architectural landmark.

We knew very little of the world beyond our own boundaries. You knew no more really than what was happening locally or what you'd see in the newspapers. Whatever was happening in the outside world, you'd hear a bit about it on the radio.

And it was through the radio that I became hooked on boxing. You could get the BBC Light Programme on our wireless and as a young lad, it was an absolute wonder to me that I could hear the live commentaries on all the big British fights of the day in our kitchen at home in Mayo. The excitement of it! And it was made even more special by the fact that an Irishman, the famous Eamonn Andrews, was often doing the commentaries. I can remember being absolutely beside myself with excitement when the English challenger Don Cockell took on the mighty Rocky Marciano for the heavyweight title of the world in 1955. It was the day after my eighth birthday. The heavyweight champion of the world was a God in those days and people had a love affair with boxing back then that has all but disappeared now. I have children and grandchildren and they'd have no interest in it whatsoever. But I devoured all I could about the sport from magazines and newspapers. If there was a fight going out live on the radio, I was glued to it. I knew by heart the champion in every weight category. Less than a fortnight after the Marciano–Cockell fight, I cried a boy's salt tears when the Irish hero of the day, Billy 'Spider' Kelly from Derry, was beaten by the Frenchman Ray Famechon for the European featherweight title in the Donnybrook bus depot in Dublin. It was a controversial points decision; everyone Irish thought Billy was robbed. I was distraught.

When I began working in Dublin I headed to the National Stadium as often as I could for the big amateur fight nights. And when I got to visit New York, I'd make my pilgrimage to Madison Square Garden. I saw several Golden Gloves contests at the Garden. Probably the biggest fight I saw there was in 1969 between Nino Benvenutti, the Italian star, and Dick Tiger from Nigeria. I loved the whole fight scene for many decades. Unfortunately, not many people love it now.

Television wasn't part of my early childhood and when it did come to Ireland, we didn't have one for a good while. We'd go up to Cowleys pub to watch *The Virginian* or *The Fugitive*. They'd show movies in the parochial hall and there'd be plenty of excitement about that, but if you wanted to go to a proper picture house, you went to Westport, seven miles away. People were in and out to Westport all the time. It wasn't exactly a roaring metropolis at the time either, but Newport was quiet and sleepy by comparison. The village didn't wake up till nine or ten of a morning, there wasn't an awful lot of sophistication and we didn't miss it either. You'd have a bit of action on a fair day alright with people coming in to buy or sell livestock; the pubs would be doing a trade and there'd be a good buzz on the street. There was eighteen pubs in the village at one time, or eighteen licences to sell alcohol anyway; some of them might only open one day a year just to keep the licence alive.

Christy Loftus was my best mate growing up. We were both born in the month of May '47. Christy lived on Meddlicott Street. We palled around everywhere together from the road to the school to the football field. I had two first cousins a hundred yards down the road that I went round with too, the twins John and Joe McGee, sons of my uncle Josie.

Tommy Kelly was headmaster of the boys' national school. He was very friendly with my father; they had the same politics and loved the GAA and Tommy had actually played for Mayo. When I was a teenager, Tommy one day said to him, 'That lad is going to play for Mayo.' He was fairly sure of it, even if the rest of us weren't. He didn't say I was going to go to university, mind you, and with good reason! It was fairly obvious from a young age that I was more interested in kicking a ball around than sticking my head in the books. I came and went through national school without giving it much thought either way. You got up in the morning, you threw your few copybooks into your satchel and off you went to class. You came home again in the afternoon not much wiser than you went in that morning. I suppose some of the learning must have stuck but, generally, there were lots of other things you preferred to be doing.

It was more or less the same in St Mary's Secondary School. It was a new school at the time, on the Castlebar side of Newport, opened in 1956 by the Sisters of Mercy. Newport never had a secondary school before that. Students previously would have to go to the convent school in Westport or the CBS there; some went to St Jarlath's in Tuam. St Mary's catchment area took in Mulranny, ten miles away, and the hinterland in between the two villages; it was also a mixed school. But even at that, the numbers were tiny and the education fairly basic. There was only about ten in my year, evenly divided between boys and girls. The school had five teachers, a couple of nuns and a couple of civilians. The principal was Sr Mechtilde. She was no Princess Grace, I'm afraid. Mechtilde was the Sister of No Mercy.

I had an aptitude for maths and could have done honours for the Leaving Cert, but there was no one to teach the subject to that level. There was no science taught either. You had the bare quota of subjects to cover and I tipped away at them, better at some than at others. English and me didn't get on great. I actually failed it in the Leaving, but thankfully that didn't matter when it came to applying for the Gardaí. In my opinion, no one should ever feel ashamed for failing a subject in their exams or for failing the whole thing altogether. There's more than one type of intelligence; academic ability is great to have, but there are other kinds of intelligence that will serve you well in life too. And there's a long life to be lived after your Leaving Cert is over; it shouldn't define anybody.

Despite my troubles with Shakespeare and the other writers on the curriculum, I ended up acting in a play in the parochial hall. It was 1966, the fiftieth anniversary of the Easter Rising, and the local drama group decided to dramatise the story of Joseph Mary Plunkett and his fiancée Grace Gifford. Every child was taught about Joseph Mary marrying Grace the night before he was executed by the British in Kilmainham Gaol. Jack Corbett was the local pharmacist and very involved with the drama society. Jack decided he needed a tall fella to play the part of Plunkett and apparently I fitted the bill. Grace was played by Margaret Neilus, long since gone to her eternal reward. I had to propose to Margaret on stage, then get married and seal it with a kiss before I was brought out to be shot. We couldn't stop laughing during the rehearsals. Anyway, it ran for a couple of nights; the crowds came to

see it and by all accounts, it was a great success. I must
have managed to learn my lines okay but, unfortunately, I
didn't manage to learn enough of them in the classroom.
If you could have studied the noble art of pugilism for the
Leaving, I'd have got an A in honours.

My class did produce a few bright sparks all the
same, one of them the aforementioned Christy Loftus,
who became a distinguished journalist with the *Western
People*, president of the National Union of Journalists
and an author. Another of our contemporaries was Denis
Coghlan who, in a long career in newspapers, became
political correspondent for *The Irish Times*.

The school didn't survive long. Newport itself only had
a population of about 600 and overall, there just weren't
enough people to keep it viable. It closed in 1969. In all
honesty, I didn't leave much of a mark on it and it didn't
leave much of a mark on me – apart from Sr Mechtilde;
she left a few marks on me alright.

There was never any pressure from the parents to
perform well at exams so as soon as I had my homework
done of an evening, I was out the door playing handball
or football or swimming in the sea. We'd be in the water
every day of the summer. You'd be on the bog too bringing
in the turf, or in the garden weeding – a job I hated. As
I got older, the sea became a source of pocket money. I
started harvesting the wrack too. In summertime you'd
go down to the bottom of the shore where it would pile
up on the big rocks and you'd cut it and bring it in with a
pitchfork and spread it out to dry on the top of the shore.
Then I'd get one of the lads with a tractor, heave it onto the

transport box and bring it to the seaweed factory. You'd get a nice few pound for a good load; it was weighed by the hundred weight, and you were paid accordingly. As a result, I was never stuck for a few bob. I saved what I could, but I always had money in my pocket. There was one drapery shop in the town, Kelly's, and they clothed all the families in the locality, often on credit where necessary. My mother would buy all our clothes in Kelly's on credit and pay it off in instalments. When I started earning my own money, I'd go into Kelly's and pay the bills. It was very much appreciated by my mother and father.

But, mark my words, it still didn't buy you any special favours with Dad. He was a disciplinarian and if there was messing going on, he wouldn't be long sorting it out. If you tried cheating at the cards, for example, you'd be thrown out of the game fairly lively. I was on the receiving end of the belt more than once! I maintain it was because of my ginger hair and the lanky set of me; I always stood out a mile. I was with a bunch of the lads one time and we were doing knick-knocks, running around knocking on doors, and one of the lads broke the glass in a door and naturally we all scattered in every direction. But who did the woman of the house spot? She spotted the tall, red-haired lad and duly reported me to Charlie McGee for breaking the glass pane. I protested my innocence, and I actually was innocent of this charge, but I was convicted without trial or jury and promptly got a few lashes of the belt. He was a strict man.

And he was straight as an arrow. Things were done right and conscientiously. He had a moral code, a strong

sense of right and wrong. There'd be no shortcuts and nothing improper. For example, he was a member of the parish hall committee and would often be on door duty for plays and dances and concerts and the like. He was trusted 100 per cent to do a job like that. Teresa tells a story about a play being on there one night and wanting to go to it, herself and her sisters and friends. It cost sixpence in old money to get in, but they reckoned that Daddy would let them in on the nod. So up she goes to the door and Dad asks her has she got her sixpence. 'No.' 'Well you better go home so.' He sent her home, wouldn't let her in.

I think I got my sense of right and wrong from him. I could never abide dishonesty. Maybe that's why I ended up doing the job I did. I had a reputation for being straight down the line. I didn't like people who were always ducking and diving and trying to pull a stroke here or a stroke there. I liked things to be done by the book and without fear or favour. A lot of times it wasn't convenient. You wouldn't be popular with people all the time with an attitude like that, but I didn't mind. I hope I was flexible and fair too. I think I was, but my instinct generally was to do the right and proper thing.

Dad died suddenly of meningitis in 1980; he was sixty-six. My mother died in 1992; she was seventy-seven. They were good people. My sister Kathleen remembers the night our father was taken to the hospital in Castlebar, having never been in hospital in his life. His red setter, Glen, whimpered at the back door that night. He normally stayed in the shed, but he wanted in this night, so one of us opened the door and let him in. He went straight up the stairs to my father's empty bedroom, saw no one there and returned outside to his shed. When my father died a few days later, Glen spent most of the night howling, obviously knowing that his master had gone to his reward.

2

TEMPLEMORE

'What about the guards?' my father used to say to me. 'You have the height for it anyway.'

It was definitely an option. I thought about being a salesman too, with the company car and the good suit and the bit of glamour about it. The army cadets as well. There was huge prestige if you 'got the cadets'. There was the bank and the civil service too, but neither really appealed to me. And joining the priesthood wasn't going to happen either. But the one thing I definitely didn't want to do was emigrate. Half of Mayo was in England or America, half of Ireland was abroad somewhere. But I wouldn't be joining them if I could help it. I wanted to make a life for myself in my own country if it could be done at all.

Early in 1966 I applied for the cadets, but it didn't work out. Dental care wasn't a big thing in post-war Ireland and I failed the medical examination for the army because I had dentures in the top part of my mouth and partial dentures on the bottom. You could say I snatched defeat from the jaws of victory, once they opened them and took a look inside. The gas thing was, I knew a fella who wore glasses who got into the cadets at the time. I never understood how a fella with glasses could be more beneficial in a war zone than a fella with dentures, especially on a rainy day. Anyway, a career in the military was out.

My father was still keen on me applying for the guards. His best friend was a member of the force at the time – Joe Meaney, I think he was a superintendent – and they were so friendly that he asked Joe to be my godfather when I was born. So he brought me in to Newport garda station to fill out the application form. A man by the name of Kealy was sergeant there at the time. Sgt Kealy measured me with a tape and obviously there was no problem with the height requirement. I was six foot two and the minimum threshold was five foot nine. The only concern he had was that I wasn't broad enough in the chest. I was a skinny lad, maybe twelve and a half stone, so there wasn't much meat on the bones. I think Sgt Kealy added an inch or two to my official chest measurement on the form. He said it didn't matter because I'd played for the Mayo minors the previous year and they'd take that into consideration. Being a county minor was a far better indication of your all-round physical fitness than your chest measurement. And I'd have no problem filling out once I got doing the gym work in Templemore. If I got to Templemore.

Sgt Kealy sent off the application form and a few weeks later I got a reply inviting me to sit the Garda entrance exam in Galway in June 1966. I wasn't the only one from my neck of the woods to do the exam. Noel McLoughlin from Westport and John Gilger from

Bofeenaun, both friends of mine, had also been invited to sit on the same day. John had a car and we all travelled together to Galway. The exam papers, as I recall, were on English, Irish and maths. All three of us passed and were duly called to the medical and the interview at the Garda depot in the Phoenix Park. This must have been around September of the same year.

I'd only been to Dublin once before I think, for a big game in Croke Park. I didn't know my way around at all. So I got a lift up with a neighbour the day before and stayed in a B&B on the North Circular Road, only a few hundred yards from the Park. I don't remember a single iota from the interview or the medical, but a few weeks later a letter landed home in Newport in the official brown envelope. And lo and behold, they'd accepted me. I was in. I was joining the Garda Síochána. I'd be heading for the training college the first week in November.

Peter had acquired a car by then, the first in the family to do so, a small Mini. He drove me to Templemore on the day, the two of us folded into the front seats and a massive suitcase containing all my clothes and PE gear and everything else in the back. I was lonesome heading off that morning, I must say, with the mother and father and my sisters waving to me. Tom Jones had a massive hit that year with *The Green, Green Grass of Home* and that was the song that kept running round in my head during the first weeks that I was away from home.

It was a long drive on bad roads in winter weather. Peter dropped me off in the college and had to turn and head back for Mayo. All the new recruits were gathered together in the assembly hall where we were addressed by the superintendent and an inspector named Fitzgerald. One of the things we were told was that we couldn't leave the campus without their permission and if we did get permission, we'd have to be back by 11 p.m. In all the excitement and nervousness, we mustn't have been listening because later that evening myself and my new roommates, Willie Mortell from Limerick and Christy McKiernan from Leitrim, decided we'd go out to see a film in the picture house at the back of the training college. It was right beside us so, in our innocence, we must've thought it'd be okay. We got back well before the 11 p.m. deadline and headed to our room. Next thing there was a loud knock on the door. Standing there with a face like thunder on him was Inspector Fitzgerald. We would discover in the next few days that he was known widely by the nickname 'Jobber'. And we would find out too that he was a bit of a head banger in his own right.

He confronted us and questioned us and his mood was not good. What authority did we have to leave the grounds without his permission? He repeated the question a couple of times. We stuttered and stammered and said we thought it was okay as long as we were back before 11 p.m. But he told us in no uncertain terms that it was not okay. In fact, he told us there and then that we were dismissed. We'd be gone in the morning. Well, Jesus, the shock of it. We didn't sleep a wink that night. Christy had been in England and said he'd go back to England. But I didn't know how I was going to go home and face my family again. You'd never live it down. Willie Mortell,

God rest him, was in the same boat as me. We were fecking mortified.

We went down to breakfast the next morning and we were all brought out to do our first parade and every minute we were expecting Fitzgerald to tap us on the shoulder and tell us to pack our bags. But he never did. He didn't come near us. We were on tenterhooks for several days before we could relax again. It had been a warning to us, a ferocious warning.

We paraded in our Garda uniforms every morning; that was part of the daily routine. There was plenty of marching. You had PE classes every day and the academic stuff mainly concentrated on legislation and Acts of Parliament. It was all new to us. Learning about your powers of arrest was a critical part of your studies. You had to get that right. The fear of arresting a person wrongly or not citing the relevant Act was something that never really left me; it filtered right through my career in the guards. You are taking away someone's liberty so you better know what you're doing.

We didn't get out at weekends. There wasn't a lot to do. You had the handball alley and the swimming pool and you could do all the exercise you wanted. On Sundays you were marched in formation to Mass. Those times, it was never even questioned but that you'd to go Mass on Sunday. If we had a choice in the matter, I don't recall us being told about it. I don't know what the story would have been if you were Church of Ireland or an atheist or whatever; it was just assumed that everyone would go to Mass. I didn't question it at all. It was just something that you did from childhood. And anyway, my faith has always been important to me; I was happy to say my prayers and I still do, more or less every day.

We were in the training college for eighteen weeks. In hindsight it wasn't near enough time. You'd gone in there totally raw, a country boy, and you were churned out eighteen weeks later; you were supposed to be a comprehensively trained policeman by the time you left. Obviously, you'd learn a lot more when you went on the job; that's where everyone learns in every line of work, but I think we should have had more time in training to get a better grounding in all aspects of the career that awaited you.

A few days prior to the passing-out parade, you were told what station you were being assigned to. And for some reason at the time, the tallest fellas in the class would be assigned as a matter of rote to Pearse Street in Dublin. There were fifty fellas in the class – no Bean Gardaí – and the tallest cohort would be sent to Pearse Street. I was one of them, albeit I wasn't the tallest; a few other lads were touching 6'3" and 6'4". Apparently, the thinking was that if you were in a busy city centre station in Dublin with thousands of people milling around, you'd be easier seen if you were tall. The Garda presence would be more visible on the streets. But as I understand it, that reasoning only applied to Pearse Street and not the other city centre stations. Anyway, mine wasn't to reason why; you just did what you were told and went where you were sent.

The recruits in my class were from all over Ireland. Actually, there were very few Dubs. The guards was traditionally a rural police force. I don't know why; maybe it had something to do with fellas being reared on bacon and cabbage! But the force was full of big country lads and sure I was just another one of them. It has changed completely since then and nowadays there are loads of Dublin lads and lassies in blue, and that's a very good thing. One of the Dubs we did have in Pearse Street was a great character and colleague, George Power. George was a driver, and he used to have this theory, if you could call it a theory, about the difference between a Dub and a culchie. He always maintained that 'You could give a Dublin man a kick in the backside and tell him to go home and he'd go home. But you could give a country man a kick in the backside and tell him to go home and he wouldn't; he'd stand there waiting for a second one.'

In March 1967, we had our passing-out parade and we were scattered to the four corners, although I would go on to work with some of my classmates in Pearse Street, and meet many more of them again in other stations around town. There was always that camaraderie between us, having started together on this new adventure and having lived together and trained together and finally graduated together. Life of course got in the way in the coming decades for all of us, with marriages and children and work and moving around to different parts of the city and country. But we had a twenty-fifth anniversary reunion and then a fiftieth anniversary reunion and thank God we were most of us still alive to see the day and tell the tales.

After graduation, I packed my bags – and I'm glad to say I packed them eighteen weeks after Jobber told me to pack them! Pearse Street station would be my next port of call. I was on my way to Dublin for my first working day as a policeman – and indeed, the first day of the rest of my life.

3

EARLY DAYS IN PEARSE STREET

I wasn't long on the job, just a matter of weeks. I was on foot patrol around O'Connell Bridge when I saw a commotion, a crowd of people gathering at the Liffey wall and looking down at the river. I went over and took a look myself. And there below was a guard in a boat pushing a dead body with an oar. It was floating on the surface and he was nudging it in front of him, from the Eden Quay side to the Burgh Quay side.

As I made my way across the bridge, an ambulance and fire brigade arrived. By this stage, the body was floating at the bottom of the steps built into the wall. A couple of firemen descended the steps carrying a stretcher. One of them grabbed the trailing arm of the corpse to pull it towards him. The arm came away from the shoulder and the fireman fell back on his backside. Obviously, it had been in the water long enough to start decomposing. The body was clothed so the fireman wouldn't have known what state it was in at that stage. He had just applied a grip on the arm to haul the body in; he was leaning forward and when the limb detached, back he went on his backside. I was above on the footpath looking down at the scene; I got a fair old gunk when I saw this happening, I can tell you.

Eventually they got the body onto the stretcher, up the steps and into the ambulance, which brought it to the city morgue. I went back to the station, just two minutes' walk away. I'd say I was still white in the face when I got back and told them the story. The veterans in there didn't bat an eyelid at the gory details. They were far more taken up by the subplot of the guard in the rowing boat. That was the main story for them. And it was an early lesson for me of how things operate on the factory floor, so to speak, as opposed to the theory in the Training College – the wheels within wheels that become part of the culture in any big organisation.

A few of my older colleagues who also witnessed it from the Liffey wall recognised the officer in the boat. He was a senior enough guard in Store Street, on the other side of the river. And basically, what he'd done by pushing the body over to Burgh Quay was save himself a lot of work. Once the body was retrieved and taken onto dry ground on our side, we would have to do the investigation and the paperwork. Pearse Street was 'B' District, Store Street was 'C' District. We had responsibility now to try and identify the body, notify relatives if we could find them, establish cause of death from the State pathologist and do up the report. It fell to muggins here to do the report. I didn't mind, but the lads in the station who'd been around a few years knew that yer man from Store Street had pulled a fast one on us – and they weren't too happy about it. I cannot remember anything about the poor divil we found that day. Unfortunately, he was just another one of those lost souls who are found in water from time to time and it becomes our job to find out who they were and try to return them to their families so they'll get a Christian burial. It offers some kind of closure for the grieving family; their loved one has been found, they can visit his/her final resting place and put flowers on the grave.

I was starting to learn the geography of the city by then. It was important that you got a map in your mind because the city itself was your place of work – your front-line place of work at any rate. And on my very first day on the beat, I learned fairly quickly that you needed to know where you were going as well as what you were doing. Not just for your own sake but the public as well. I realised that if people saw you in uniform, they expected you to be able to give them directions. They were always looking for directions.

Sgt Michael O'Connor checked us in on the day we arrived in Pearse Street. There were four different units, one for the early shift (6 a.m.–2 p.m.), the day shift (2 p.m.–10 p.m.), night shift (10 p.m.–6 a.m.), and the resting unit. He allocated us to our different units and I was placed under the charge of two very good men, Sgt John Guest from Tipperary and Sgt Tom Mullaney from Roscommon. O'Connor was a Mayo man. We rookies had been used to a very regimental kind of set-up in Templemore: you had to wear black or navy socks with your uniform and if you wore any other colour, you'd soon know all about it. Now here was Michael and when he was addressing us, he put his foot up on a chair and lo and behold, he was wearing white socks! We thought he was a very trendy chap altogether.

I was escorted on my first patrol by an experienced man from Monaghan, Eugene Kirke. We were walking nearby the station on Townsend Street, which runs parallel to Pearse Street. Soon enough we came across a truck jammed under the railway bridge on Townsend Street. So we had to start diverting traffic and while we were doing it, motorists were rolling down their windows and asking how they were going to get from A to B now. Eugene was well able to tell them but, next thing, there was a traffic collision on Tara Street and Eugene had to leave our scene to attend that one. This left me diverting the traffic on my own and dealing with a lot of irate drivers wondering how they were going to get to Ringsend or Blackrock or wherever the hell they were going. And I didn't even know the name of the street I was standing on!

My first few months, in fact, were mostly taken up with traffic. I was put on point duty on O'Connell Bridge and learned the ropes with a few older colleagues. O'Connell Street was the busiest thoroughfare in the country, but you learned to liaise with the other guards on O'Connell Street and on the various bridges and gradually you saw how the flow of traffic worked in conjunction with your colleagues. It was a question of timing really and once you got the hang of it, you were away on a hack. But there were some fellas who could never get the hang of it; they'd make a hash of it no matter how often they tried.

We lived above the shop in those days. The new recruits were billeted in rooms above the station. You had about fifteen rooms upstairs and you could have any number between two and eight in each room. You had a steel bed and it was okay; you could get a night's sleep in it, but there were always fellas coming and going from one shift or another. The shift work played puck with your sleep patterns. One of the rules was that if you were on day shift, you had to be in bed before 12 midnight, I think to stop fellas arriving in with a load of beer on them and waking up the lads trying to get a night's kip. Even if you were off duty you had to be in bed before midnight. There was a canteen downstairs where you could get your breakfast, dinner and tea. You got paid every week and the cost of food and lodgings was deducted automatically from your salary.

I preferred to be dealing with people rather than cars and pretty soon you were starting to get to know the community that lived around you. Needless to say, it was a totally different environment to the one I'd grown up in. It was built-up, heavily populated and poor. Inevitably there was a busy caseload, albeit mainly about minor crimes. There was two big blocks of flats beside us, Pearse House and Markievicz House, and you'd be in and out of them a lot, helping the detectives search for stolen goods and the like. There were young lads breaking into cars and offices and stealing property. Naturally enough they didn't like you coming into their homes and searching for stuff and asking them questions. So we were classified as the enemy.

To try and break down those barriers, we did a lot of volunteer work, helping out the local clergy who were working in the community or various charity organisations. You could be doing door duty at a local disco in the community centre and actually, I remember a young musician and singer playing at those discos who would go on to become an international rock star only a few years later – the great Phil Lynott. It was a form of social work we were doing I suppose, trying to keep the kids off the streets and getting to know them and trying to mentor them in some small way. But there was rarely any serious crime that you had to deal with. There wasn't any serious violence or dangerous situations that I can recall. Families were living in cramped conditions, parents were struggling to bring in enough money, it wasn't an easy task to keep teenagers on the straight and narrow all the time.

We had a juvenile liaison section that operated out of the station and it was headed up by Sgt Tom Casey and Garda Jack Dunne. We were shocked many years later to discover Jack was a paedophile who'd used his role to target children and abuse them. What's more, he did it repeatedly in Pearse Street station. He had a room of his own there. We thought he was doing great work at the time. You'd often see him with three or four boys in the canteen and giving them breakfast or lunch and chatting away to them. We thought he was an exceptionally charitable, compassionate man. And he was very friendly and amenable as a colleague. If you asked him for a favour, he'd do whatever he could to help. But it turned out he was bringing boys up to his room and exploiting them atrociously. He got away with it for years. Dunne was also the leader of a boy scout troop and had preyed upon dozens of children in this role too.

As I understand it, he left the Garda force in the mid-late 1970s and it must have been under a cloud because by then, he'd only have been in his early forties. I had left Pearse Street well before that so never heard anything about the reasons for his leaving. The only thing I knew about him around that time was that he'd joined a religious order, the Congregation of the Blessed Sacrament. And we all knew about that because he ended up saying Mass in the famous Blessed Sacrament chapel on D'Olier Street, just round the corner from the station.

The truth about Jack Dunne finally poured out in a series of court cases in the early 2010s, when he was successfully prosecuted for historic crimes of child abuse. It had been a campaign of terror over many years, usually perpetrated on boys in their early teens or younger. Multiple victims came forward to tell their stories. Six new victims came forward after he was jailed in 2013. They were waiting for their day in court when Dunne died the following year, at the age of eighty-three. Sadly, those victims, and probably many more, never got the justice they deserved.

* * *

Your first two years on the job were your probationary period. You were officially a recruit Garda during that time. Thankfully I learned the ropes without blotting my copybook and generally got through it without any bother at all. Better still, I was really enjoying the work: the variety of it, being out and about, the craic and the camaraderie; it all suited me down to the ground. Reports were filed intermittently by your superiors about your ongoing progress. The only time I might have had a negative entry in my record was down to a nit-picking senior officer up in the Phoenix Park.

The 1970s saw a general increase in illegal drug use in Dublin and for the first time a dedicated unit – the drug squad – was set up to tackle the problem. It was led by the experienced Detective Inspector Denis Mullins and initially consisted of ten male detectives. As time progressed, so did the squad, with the addition of females and trained surveillance officers, all of which made it more successful in fighting the war against drugs which is still waging, not alone in the capital but all over the country.

November 1972 saw the biggest drugs raid to date, when thirty-six Gardaí, both uniform and detective, led a bust on the Yeoman Inn on South King Street, off Stephen's Green. This operation saw a hundred people being searched, of whom thirty-four were arrested and twenty-one charged. The raid, which took place at 9 p.m. on a Saturday night, came about after detectives had kept the premises under surveillance day and night for fourteen days. It was believed by both the Gardaí and the public that the pub was a popular place to both score and take illegal drugs. Cannabis, marijuana and LSD were found littered on the ground, dropped by punters when they realised what was going on, while drugs were also found hidden in the toilets, behind piping and wooden beams and in dustbins. The drug squad detectives told journalists that after the 'lightning crackdown' they expected the drugs scene in the city would 'become very quiet'.

The drug squad were raiding the Yeoman again another day. Myself and Ollie Hanley from Roscommon were there to provide support. Ollie was one of my classmates from Templemore. A press photographer turned up at the scene; I presume he'd got a tip-off that a raid was going down. A crowd gathered on the street outside the pub as the detectives did their business inside. And in one of the next day's newspapers, wasn't there a picture of the crowd outside – and there's me and Ollie in the middle of it. The only problem was that I wasn't wearing my Garda cap and Ollie had his hand in his pocket. I had left my cap back in

the patrol car. And some bright spark up in the Headquarters in the Phoenix Park with nothing better to be doing saw this photo and decided that we should be investigated.

There was a certain kind of inspector or super who loved sitting at his desk and doing sweet feck all except flexing his authority. And one of these smartasses decided that we should be disciplined for breaches of uniform etiquette and deportment. The rules were that I should have my cap on me at all times to identify myself as a guard, and a member shouldn't be going around with his hands in his pockets. But he couldn't discipline you without first of all getting a report of the incident. And our sergeant on the day got us off the hook. The detectives had been getting a bit of hassle from the crowd as they conducted the raid and myself and Ollie moved in to quell any aggro. It was only a little bit of a shemozzle, nothing much to it at all, but our sergeant put it in his report that my cap had been knocked off and Ollie had his hand in his pocket because he was taking out the keys of the car! We heard no more from that genius above in the Park.

Working the beat was often boring, but sometimes boredom could turn to amusement in the most peculiar ways. One night while on my own in Fleet Street I was accosted by a gang of eight to ten ladies out on a hen party. They were in great form as they proceeded to manhandle or womanhandle me. Some of them jumped up on my back, others ran their hands all over my uniform, while my cap left my head and my whistle left my tunic pocket. My cap was hurled up in the air a few times before it was returned to me and I had to plead to get my whistle back. When order was restored, they went on their merry way and I'm sure they relayed their happy two minutes with the young Garda many times to their friends, if they remembered it. I remember it quite vividly to this day and have relived it many times with fondness.

With your two years' probation done, you were sent back to Templemore where you'd do a refresher course to brighten up your knowledge of the laws and after that, you were no longer a recruit guard. The L plates were off, you were officially a guard.

After that, you moved out of the station and found a place to live. Myself and Pat Morgan from Clare and Willie Gallagher from Roscommon – Willie played on the Ros county team for a few years – moved into a flat on Harcourt Street. Now it wasn't a palace. It had a ferocious high roof on it and it was awful hard to keep it warm, but it was better than the station anyway.

At this stage, I was an official driver. I'd passed my driving test, and when we were on a month of nights, we would have the job of patrolling the city in a Bedford van. And it was on these nightly excursions that I first came across the legend that was Sergeant Jim Branigan. And he truly was a legend by then. Jim would've been pushing sixty at that stage, but he was still strong as an ox and still mad for road. He was the most famous guard in Ireland, maybe the only famous guard in Ireland, and to everyone far and wide he was known as 'Lugs' Branigan. But I never called him that and you didn't dare call him that. He'd got the nickname from some criminal or other back in the day because of his big ears and it was a very sore point with him. You did not, under any circumstances, call him Lugs. He was Jim or 'Branno'. Jim travelled in a van around the city at night too, Bravo 5, but in the job, the van was known as 'Branno 5'.

Jim always worked the night shift and on my month of nights I worked in tandem with him and I drove another van, Bravo 3, in support. If word came through on the radio that Branno 5 needed back-up at a scene, you'd be there as fast as you could press the accelerator. Often there'd be some sort of melee going off in a dance hall or outside a dance hall and Branno would need assistance taking prisoners.

On Benburb Street one night there was a guard in trouble, and myself and my colleague arrived in Bravo 3 to help him. We took a prisoner by the name of Gillespie down to the Bridewell. There was no screen between the front seats and the rear space in the vans, those days. My colleague was in the back with the prisoner, but Gillespie was an awful big strong fella and he was angry too, shouting and roaring and trying to burst out through the back door. My man was struggling to keep a hold of him and I was reaching back with my free arm trying to get a grip of him too, only I ended up getting the end of his shoe in my face. I put my hand up to my cheek and there was blood on it. Gillespie was still flailing away so I climbed into the back and there were punches and kicks flying until we finally got him subdued. In hindsight, I don't think the kick to my face was deliberate, he was just demented with drink and anger and was lashing out indiscriminately, but we had to meet fire with fire to get him down on the floor and keep him there until we got to the Bridewell.

The only problem was, nobody in the station wanted to charge him. He was battered and bruised from the fracas and the guards on duty knew that if they charged him, he'd be bringing a charge of assault against us. Branno was working that night and we radioed him. He came straight to the Bridewell and declared, 'I'll charge him, I'll charge him no problem at all.' And he duly did and turned up in court next day with the prisoner. That was the way he operated and such was the power of his reputation, he knew his word would go a long way to persuading any judge in any court. If a defence lawyer stood up and said his client had been ill-treated while in custody, and there was marks on him to prove it, Branigan would openly declare that the prisoner only got enough to keep him quiet and put manners on him. The likes of me couldn't say that to a judge – I'd be too embarrassed to say it – but he'd say it straight up.

Jim was proud of his reputation as a one-man riot squad. You'd meet him at night – he only ever worked nights – as it suited him and ordinarily the riot squad would rarely be required during the day.

I never saw him with a baton in his hand ever. I rarely used it either. You always had it in your pocket but I seldom ever drew it. You had all sorts of rules and regulations in relation to when you could use it and why and how. Jim had a pair of black leather gloves and they were his weapon. If a fella was giving him lip, he'd get a smack of the gloves and if the same fella had drink taken, or didn't know any better, he'd say, 'Ah Jaysus, Lugs, there's no need for that.' And then he'd get another smack of them for

calling the great man by his nickname. He often started
rows himself, the fecker, cos he didn't like backchat and
if someone gave him backchat, that chap would be eating
leather soon enough. You might be at a shemozzle outside
somewhere like the Olympic ballroom or the National and
we'd have gotten it quietened down until Branno arrived
and someone called him 'Lugs' and next thing, smack!
Straightaway in with the smack of the gloves.

Saying that, I never saw him get involved in any out-
and-out brawling either. That would be far too unseemly
and he had far too much respect for himself to be getting
involved in street melees like that. And he wouldn't wade
into a row unless he knew he had back-up behind him. It
was often to do with fellas resisting arrest and he'd need
support getting them bodily off the street and into the
back of the van. Bear in mind that he was a man of sixty
or thereabouts, still out there on the streets and still facing
down whatever was coming his way from fellas who
were half his age. Mind you, he had got good support
too from his right-hand man in those years, one Tom
'Sonny' Heaney. Sonny was 6'3" and a former tug-of-war
champion. He had plenty of power if it was needed. Jim
retired from the force in 1973 and died in 1986. On the
day of the annual Garda Sportstar Awards in November
2014, word came through that Sonny had died. Alan
Quinlan, the former Munster and Ireland rugby player,
was doing MC that night. I was there to receive the Hall
of Fame award. Alan, in his speech, joked about being
a bit of a tearaway in his teenage years, saying it was a
funny turn of events that he was speaking now at this

prestigious Garda function. Said I to Alan, when I went up to get my award, if Jim Branigan and Sonny Heaney had come across him back then, they wouldn't have been long straightening him out!

But in actual fact Jim was a far more rounded individual than the hard man of public renown. I can put my hand on my heart and tell anyone that he was one decent human being. There's no doubt that he took the law into his own hands at times. That can't be denied. But he had been a boxing man all his life; an amateur champion and then for decades a boxing referee. He knew what it was like to stand inside the four ropes of a boxing ring. And he had the mentality of a boxer; you stood toe-to-toe with someone and sorted it out there and then with a few punches. But you kept your discipline and you didn't beat a man when he was down. You did enough, as he said, to put manners on him in the old-fashioned way. If a fella ended up in court with a black eye, so be it. And I know he did many a good turn for fellas who ended up tangling with him. He gave lots of lads a second chance and a third chance. If he got talking to a defence lawyer and heard a bit about the client's back story, he'd often try to help out rather than just get the lad convicted. He had compassion and a sense of decency.

I know his style of policing went out with the ark but, in my opinion, there was a lot to be said for it then, and maybe there's a lot to be said for it now. We have a desperate amount of crime on our streets nowadays and far as I can see, there's too many do-gooders always looking to defend the rights of the perpetrator rather than the victim.

Personally, I found him to be a lovely man. We got on great despite the generation gap between us. He had a big interest in the GAA and loved talking to me about football and how I was getting on with Mayo and all that. I had the greatest of respect for him as a man and a Garda. He commanded respect in the courts, among local councillors and politicians, in the business community, on the streets and in the police force. And I mean, he is still being talked about nearly fifty years after he retired. TG4 had a documentary on him only a few years ago. It was a privilege to have worked with him because in Dublin city, once upon a time, Jim Branigan was lord of the rings.

4

FOUR GOAL McGEE

As a teenager and back in those early years with An Garda Síochána, there was another thing which took up a fair bit of my time – I had something of a passion and flare for football – and it is an amazing thing to me that what happened in one particular match in 1967 still follows me around to this day, fifty-five years later and counting. It gave me a pet nickname that people still use when they greet me and, in the decades since, I can't count the number of times that I've been introduced to people as Willie 'Four Goal' McGee. At the time I had no clue that it would be remembered at all, much less that it would last this long.

It was 8 October of that year, the All-Ireland under-21 final. Mayo were playing Kerry in a replay in Ballinasloe. The conditions were desperate. It had rained all morning and it was still raining hard when the match started; the pitch was heavy with mud and water. I was selected at right corner forward. There was only about forty-five seconds gone when Tom Fitzgerald, our left half forward, lobbed a high ball in. It landed and bounced around the parallelogram; I slipped as I went for it, but as I was falling, I got a hand to it before the defenders and diverted it past the keeper.

I don't remember all the details clearly so I'll let Gerry McCarthy of *The Irish Press* describe the next one as it appeared in his match report. 'Goal No. 2 arrived in the 25th minute when Kerry, having survived an early Mayo onslaught, trailed by 0–2 to 1–4. McGee got possession 14 yards out and O'Brien never saw his left-footed rasper to the corner of the net.'

I got the third about three minutes later. John Gibbons was playing centre forward and went on a run down the right wing. The great Mayo GAA writer Seán Rice was there for the *Connaught Telegraph* that day. 'Gibbons' shot swung to the right of the goal and appeared to be going wide when a sudden flick from McGee's fist turned the ball in flight and it dropped under the body of Kerry's goalkeeper.' Another report had it that it was Seamus O'Dowd who sent in the ball, but I honestly can't remember.

All of a sudden, we were going in at half-time leading 3–4 to 0–4. But we'd led by eight points at half-time in the drawn game in Croke Park a month earlier and Kerry wiped out that lead in the second half. In fact, it took a late point from O'Dowd to save our bacon. So we were very mindful of not letting them back into it this time. Kerry never really got going at all until the final quarter when they reduced the deficit to six points with seven or eight minutes remaining. Then I got my fourth with about five minutes left and that sealed it. John D. Hickey

in the *Irish Independent* called it 'a picture goal'. It was
the pick of the bunch alright. I remember catching a high
ball, turning, selling their full back a dummy and burying
it in the net from a fair bit out. And that killed any hopes
of a Kerry comeback. The final scoreline was Mayo 4–9
Kerry 1–7. I was dubbed 'the red-haired menace' in *The
Kerryman* the following week.

My most vivid memory of the day by far is what
happened after the final whistle. A good scatter of Mayo
supporters came onto the field and next thing my father
was there giving me this big hug and he was crying. And
like most men of his generation, he wasn't the type to show
his emotions at all. He was a serious man, but here he was
with his arms around me and the tears were showing and
at first, I was wondering was there something wrong? But
he was just overcome with pride and joy. That's when it
dawned on me that I'd done something special.

But even at that, there was no big fuss afterwards. I've no memory of the cup being presented or big speeches or the like. Christy Loftus was full back; he was part of a Mayo backline that really locked down the Kerry forwards that day. And actually, we had a third club colleague on the team, Jimmy Ryan from Kilmeena who played right half back. Christy says there was a homecoming of sorts with the cup but that the players had made their own transport arrangements to get to Ballinasloe, so there was no team bus to bring everyone back together and go on a tour of the county. The squad split up after the game and fellas went in groups back to their parts of Mayo.

I went straight back to Dublin that evening. I was about six months in the job at the time so there was no question of me taking the night off to celebrate. I got back to Pearse Street station and the thing I was looking forward to most was seeing the next day's newspapers. The offices of *The Irish Times* were just round the corner on D'Olier Street, the *Irish Press* was around the other corner on Burgh Quay and the *Irish Independent* just over the Liffey bridge on Abbey Street. We always had guards bringing back early copies nearly as soon as they rolled off the printing presses around midnight. I couldn't wait to get the *Irish Press* in particular because it was the leading GAA paper of the day and of course I knew well that the family back in Newport would be getting it first thing later on Monday morning.

I went round to Burgh Quay at the appointed hour for the first edition and sure enough there was the banner headline on the sports pages: 'Four Goal McGee A Hero'.

There were variations on the same theme in the other papers. And from that day forward, my name wasn't my own! It still gets mentioned in the Mayo newspapers when they're looking back at various highlights from our footballing history. The story gets recycled over and over, often I suppose by the older generation passing it onto their children and they in turn passing it onto their own children. I've met Mayo fans young and old and in between and they've heard about it and want to ask me about it. It's a bit of craic too; people love saying to me, 'Four Goal McGee!', like it's the first time I've ever heard it. We had a fiftieth anniversary reunion in Galway in 2017 and it dominated the reminiscences on the night.

I don't really know what to say about it anymore, it's all been said. There was a team behind those goals, a good team with a lot of very good players, but they've been kind of forgotten about in the whole telling of that final. It wasn't a great game; in fact, it was a poor game played in wretched conditions, so I suppose it's just that the four goals stood out by a mile as a headline. It's not that common for a team to score four goals in a game, but it's a freak occurrence that all four would be scored by the same man. And I suppose that's why it has followed me around for the rest of my days.

I was twenty years old at the time and I was on a high that week. Two years earlier I'd experienced the worst low of my young footballing life. It turned out to be the lowest day I would ever experience on a football field. If I ever came near to proper depression, I did for this. We were hot favourites to win the Connacht minor championship of 1965. We had a brilliant team. Or we thought we did anyway. We'd absolutely destroyed Galway in the semi-final in Castlebar. We thought it was only a matter of turning up against Roscommon in the final and boy, did we learn a bitter lesson. We were raging hot favourites, but they beat us 2–10 to 1–10 in Tuam. I'd scored 1–4 against Galway. I was held scoreless against Roscommon and taken off. I was inconsolable for weeks after. I had these big dreams of going to Croke Park for the All-Ireland semi-final and getting on the television! I had it in my head that RTÉ would be showing highlights of the game and I'd score a couple of goals and make it onto the telly! But now my race was run. I'd be too old for the minors in '66 and as it happened, Mayo won the whole shooting gallery that year, Connacht and All-Ireland titles. In fact, that minor team would go on in '67 to form the backbone of our under-21 team. But the '65 minors, it haunted me for a long time after.

I'll tell you something else that haunted me too – the beating I took from Sr Mechtilde earlier that year. Myself and Christy both got it in the classroom one day a few weeks before the Leaving Cert. She had banned us from playing football coming up to the big exam. But that was impossible; we could no more not play football than not eat our dinner. What's more we were on the Mayo minor team by then. That was a big deal for two bucks from Newport. Anyway, we played a match for the minors; I think it was a Connacht league game, and of course in a parish the size of Burrishoole, word was always going to get out. So as I recall it, she asked us in class on the

Monday if we'd been playing football at the weekend.
And of course, we said no and she seemed to take our
word for it. Then the Mayo newspapers came out a day
or two later and wasn't there a write-up about the county
minor match the previous weekend with our names in
print and all. The next day she came into the classroom
again and she had the cane with her this time. She had
a face of thunder on her. And she asked Christy and me
again if we'd been playing football at the weekend. We
knew there was no denying it this time. So we admitted it
and she started raging at us. Not alone had we disobeyed
her orders, but we'd told lies about it too. And next thing
she was walloping us with the cane. She lost control of
herself, just kept whacking it down on us. By the time she
was finished with us she was red in the face and out of
breath and actually frothing at the mouth, nearly like she
was getting pleasure out of it.

For a finish, she told us we were expelled from the
school and couldn't sit our exams there. We were sent
home. Naturally there was consternation all round.
Christy's father, Bob, and my father got together and
decided to make a visit to Sr Mechtilde and plead our
case. But she wasn't for turning. So there was nothing for
it but to take it to the next level – to Archbishop Joseph
Walsh himself, the top man in the diocese of Tuam. As it
happened, Archbishop Joe was a son of Newport. He'd
have known both our families back the generations. He
was an elderly man at that stage. Anyway, our two-man
delegation made the pilgrimage to the bishop's palace in
Tuam to make their case on behalf of their errant sons.

It was a successful diplomatic mission. Phone calls were made; we were reinstated. Two years later we were back in the Mayo papers again, this time splashed all over them after bringing home the under-21 title. I don't suppose the good sister would have had too much interest in that.

But the people of the area certainly did. It was a source of great pride to have three of their own players on an All-Ireland winning team. That was a big contingent from our corner of the county. We were never one of the powerhouses of Mayo football – far from it. In fact, the Burrishoole GAA club had only been founded in 1958. Before that, Newport had its own club and at the other end of the parish was Mulranny, which used to play with Achill. Then Newport and Mulranny amalgamated to form the GAA club that would be named after the parish, Burrishoole.

Christy and me would've been about eleven years old at the time. We were already stone mad about the game. We'd been kicking a ball around since the infants' class in national school. Truth be told, there wasn't much else to be doing at the time by way of amusing ourselves. You went to school, did your homework and went out and played football and that was it. This was the time before television, never mind computer games and mobile phones and the Internet. So more or less every young fella in the school joined in too.

All the lads would gather for a kickaround in the handball alley next door during the lunch break or we'd head through the railway tunnel towards what was known as Dick's Field. There was a green area where the dispensary is now and we'd play ball on it too. On Fridays, if the weather was good, we'd be let out for an hour of football in Dick's Field. That wasn't his first name; it was his second name. Mr Dick had been a local landowner at one time. His land was later bought by the Land Commission and divided up among the local farmers, but his name stuck on this particular field. You had to go through the train tunnel under the viaduct; it's a fairly long tunnel, maybe eighty to one hundred yards long. There was no danger of getting hit by an oncoming train; they had stopped coming a good few decades earlier. The field was on the side of a hill. You threw down your jackets and jumpers for goalposts and you'd tear away at a game for the next hour and often a lot longer. Everyone joined in, the good, middling and bad, because nobody wanted to be left behind in the classroom. At that time there was no organised juvenile football until the under-15s, so everything you learned about the game, you learned it by playing in these free-for-alls in the handball alley or in Dick's Field or just out on the street with the ball in your hands. There was no coaching of any description. You did what came naturally to you and whatever natural talent you had was developed without you knowing. Catching and kicking and soloing and sidestepping and shooting were the skills you learned along the way. If you were lucky, nature had started you off with some amount of inbuilt aptitude for the skills. And if you were luckier still, nature gave you a decent amount of athletic ability to start off with too, for running and jumping, sprinting and endurance. But whatever you had, it was all developed over the hours and days and weeks and years of playing with your friends.

I played a lot of competitive handball too for a good few years. It's a tough sport – you have to be fast and fit to cover the court – and it's also brilliant for developing your hand-eye co-ordination. These were assets that you transferred without knowing to your football game as well. The other asset I developed in those teenage years was my left side. I became a two-footed kicker of the ball. Again, it was as much by accident as anything else: I injured my right foot when I was young and resorted to kicking the ball with my left an awful lot as a result. I ended up being able to use both barrels as I got older.

Anyway, in time to come, all of that natural development was enough to get Christy and me onto the Mayo minor team and to win the All-Ireland at under-21. By that stage we had graduated to the senior ranks at the club. You started going up to the club pitch when you were a teenager and playing with the adults, the big lads. You were down on the bottom rung of the ladder when you started kicking around with them; they wouldn't give you the ball too easy and you didn't have too many balls to go round either. The club might only have one good ball, maybe two, so getting your hands on it was a job in itself. We were still using the old-style leather footballs at that time; they were heavy and the seam was prone to getting stretched and torn. You wouldn't throw them away; they'd be brought to the local cobbler and he'd stitch them back together.

I needed a bit of stitching myself one time as a young

fella, maybe seventeen or eighteen. We were playing a match. I was going in after a high ball to make sure it ended up in the net. I was looking up at it instead of looking where I was going and ran straight into the upright and hopped my head off it! I was knocked out. I woke up in the hayshed. The hayshed across the road from the pitch was where we togged out in those days. They carted me over to a car and brought me to Dr O'Dea to get stitched up.

Burrishoole won West Mayo titles at junior grade in the early '60s and in 1966 myself and Christy were on the team that won the club's first intermediate county championship. Seamie Daly would have been one of the key men involved with the club in those years; he was from Mulranny. Seamie was really the first mentor we had who introduced us to a level of coaching and preparation. Christy's father-in-law Larry McGovern was another driving force that the club had in those years. He was Mr GAA in Newport. Larry went on to become chairman of the Mayo county board.

I played mostly at full forward, I was the target man for a lot of ball and as a result, the target man for a fair bit of attention from full backs. Between my height and the big ginger head on me, I stood out like a lighthouse anyway. And after '67 I had a bit of a public profile, a reputation as a goal-scoring forward, so naturally enough, defenders were always going to try and stop me one way or another. In fairness I don't recall getting any bad doings, just that there was a lot of holding and grappling and getting surrounded by backs any time the ball came near me. I didn't get into personal battles with players either. I wasn't one for retaliating or even for backchat. I tried to play the game in a fair and sporting way.

But there's one game from my club days that stands out. It was a hot and heavy affair with our local rivals Kilmaine. There was a melee between the supporters. It started with the linesman getting a clatter and next thing there were several people piling into a shemozzle on the pitch – including my own father! He had a new umbrella with him and he was wielding it. He ended up breaking it over some fella's back! It was most definitely out of character for a man who was normally so sensible and level-headed. Anyway, order was eventually restored and the game resumed. Then I got a chance. I played a one-two with a teammate, took my shot – and hit it wide. I should have scored. Next thing, I heard a comment from one of the Kilmaine supporters, a smartarse remark to the effect it was no wonder Mayo were so bad. I was on the county senior team at this stage. Anyway, not two minutes later another ball came in and there was no mistake this time. Bang. Back of the net. The Burrishoole supporters erupted and I turned and put my fist up to the smart Alec in the crowd. I never did that before; those kind of gestures to the crowd weren't the done thing in those days.

One day I called into Sheridan's supermarket on the main street in Newport to do a bit of shopping. I was greeted by the owner, Mrs Sheridan, who was accompanied by her young son John. She asked me a question, clearly for the purpose of John's attention: 'Willie, do you eat porridge every morning?' 'Of course I do,' I replied, 'it's good for you!' She looked down at John and told him that he'd have to start eating porridge if he wanted to become a good footballer like Willie McGee. A few weeks later, I visited the shop again and was informed by a delighted Mrs Sheridan that John couldn't get enough porridge every morning to satisfy his liking for the food. She was so glad that he took my advice. That same boy would grow into a healthy man who is now working in the United States.

Unfortunately, my time wearing the lily-white jersey of Burrishoole didn't last very long. I transferred to the Garda GAA club in Dublin in October 1968. Mick Connor, my sergeant in Pearse Street, had become very involved in setting up the club and so had another good colleague, Jim Murphy, and they'd been onto me about transferring almost from the time I started in the station in '67. The Garda GAA club had ceased to function a number of years before. That was one factor. But the big issue for me was the shift work and the travelling. It was an absolute killer. You could be doing a week of nights and then find yourself heading for Mayo on a Sunday morning with your sleep patterns all over the place. It often happened that you'd be doing a shift on the Saturday night, you'd fall into bed for a couple of hours, say at 6 a.m. on a Sunday morning, get maybe three hours' kip and then get up and drive west, play a match and turn around and head straight back to Dublin. It was exhausting, mentally and physically. Your head or your body wouldn't be near right for playing a game.

My first car was a Volkswagen Beetle and it was grand, but you'd be driving it, rather than it driving you. There wasn't all the creature comforts you'd have in a car nowa-days. Bad roads and bad weather meant it could take you four hours to get home. And the same back again. It just wasn't sustainable so I had to make the decision. I was still on the road a lot anyway, between playing with Mayo and going home to see the folks, but playing my club foot-ball in Dublin took a massive amount of the pressure off. I had a long association with the Garda GAA club for decades after, as a player, member and official.

There was nothing said to my face about it at the time, but I'm sure there were disappointed people in Burris-hoole when I upped sticks. My father was one of them. He didn't try to change my mind or talk me out of it, but he did say it was a pity I had to leave and I knew from the tone of his voice that he was sad about it.

Many years later, I think it was 2003, a chance meeting with the then chairman of Burrishoole, John Pat Sheridan, and the treasurer, the late Sean Chambers, resurrected my interest in the club. I proposed that I could help raise some finances for the club in the shape of a golf classic in my own club, Westmanstown. They gave me their blessing, the event was a huge success and the Burrishoole finances were in the region of €26,300 better off as a result. I continued to fundraise for a number of years afterwards and my heart is still there to this day for any support I can assist them with.

5

TAKE YOUR POINTS, THE GOALS WILL COME

In the spring of '68 I was drafted onto the Mayo senior panel. I made my league debut in April and my championship debut against Sligo in Castlebar that June. Galway beat us by a point in the Connacht final, also in MacHale Park.

In February '69 I was thrilled to get a call-up to the Connacht Railway Cup team. It was still a massively prestigious tournament for players, even though the numbers attending had been going down during the decade. But I didn't care about that at all, I was bursting with excitement at the thoughts of rubbing shoulders with the great stars of the day. We played Ulster in the semi-final in Tuam. I started on the bench. Connacht had the likes of Dermot Earley from Roscommon, Mickey Kearins from Sligo and from Galway, Noel Tierney, Jimmy Duggan and John Keenan among others. Ulster had household names from their Down contingent such as Seán O'Neill, Paddy Doherty and Joe Lennon, along

with highly respected players like Mickey Niblock from Derry and Ray Carolan from Cavan.

I was sent on in the second half. Seamus Hoare from Donegal was their goalkeeper. Seamus lives in Leixlip and he often tells the story of how, when he saw me trotting into the full forward line, he warned the Ulster backs in front of him to keep an eye on that young lad, he has an eye for a goal. And he reckons the words weren't out of his mouth when he was picking the ball out of the net! Mick Dunne was there for the *Irish Press* that day. The sides were level early in the fourth quarter. 'Then Dermot Earley sent in a short centre which McGee caught neatly, skipped around two defenders, and when it seemed he must be in trouble shot through for the best goal of the hour.' It broke the match our way. The final was against Munster, in Croke Park on St Patrick's Day as was the tradition, and we beat them handily. I started full forward and scored two points. Connacht wouldn't win another

Railway Cup until 2014, by which time it was on its last legs as a tournament.

Winning the Railway Cup was nice, in and of itself, but the real bonanza was a trip to New York, all expenses paid, to partake in the Cardinal Cushing Games. It was a fantastic experience – my first time in America. We had an absolute ball. We played a series of games in Gaelic Park, against New York and teams from Boston and Hartford, Connecticut. In Hartford, as we ran out onto the pitch, two of our players barely made it a few steps before falling over. They were suffering from the effects of too much alcohol the night before and were substituted straightaway, with no observer being any the wiser as to why they had been replaced.

At a celebratory function after the match we met Fr Peter Quinn, who was a member of the Mayo All-Ireland-winning teams of 1950 and 1951 and who was now based in a diocese in Connecticut. Peter was the third last member of those winning teams to pass away.

I made some great friends on that trip and to this day I have a lovely photo of the six guards in our white Connacht jerseys who made the trip: myself, John Morley and Johnny Carey from Mayo, Cathal Cawley from Sligo, Noel Colleran from Galway, and Dan O'Grady, who was also from Mayo but played with Leitrim.

In those years there was also an annual tournament in Wembley Stadium, no less, involving the top hurling and Gaelic football teams of the day, and I was lucky enough to make a couple of those shindigs to London too. They were usually played on the Whit bank holiday weekend.

It was an amazing experience to play at one of the most famous stadiums in all of world sport. The facilities alone would leave you with your mouth open. They had these massive dressing rooms, really plush and comfortable, with a big plunge pool or communal bath for soaking in after a game. And as for the pitch itself, it was like playing on a green carpet. For fellas who grew up togging out in haysheds and ditches by the side of the road, it was a whole different world.

In the '69 senior championship we faced Galway again in the Connacht final in Pearse Stadium and were steeped to get a replay out of it. Galway were leading by two well into the last quarter when they somehow made a hash of an open goal. Pat Donnellan got in behind the cover. He had Liam Sammon with him. They had only the keeper to beat. Donnellan's shot rolled past Eugene Rooney, Sammon ran in to make sure of it, or maybe just to hammer it into the back of the net for effect; either way it was only inches from crossing the line. Incredibly, he got his feet in a muddle and ended up standing on the ball and stopping it and Rooney managed to scramble back and clear it. It was an unbelievable let-off. And they hit about ten wides too. We took full advantage in the replay two weeks later in Castlebar.

That was on 3 August; we didn't have much time to get our heads around it and prepare for the All-Ireland semi-final; the following Sunday we were out against Kerry in Croke Park. Final score: Kerry 0–14 Mayo 1–10. We had the saving of it; we could and should have brought it to a replay. According to Paddy Downey's match report in

The Irish Times, Kerry were a good bit the better team and deserved to win. But they'd missed a load of chances. They'd hit the crossbar twice midway through the first half with goal-bound shots, and kicked wide after wide in the second half. We were actually level at half-time, but Kerry's superiority eventually told on the scoreboard and they led by five points with ten minutes to play.

But we rallied; Des Griffith scored a terrific goal and the comeback was on. Kerry were suddenly rattled. I was playing right corner forward and getting onto a load of ball; I was getting fouled a lot too. 'Panic was perceptible among the Kerry backs,' reported Downey, and they 'indulged in their share of the pull-down'. I had scored two points from play and the fella that was marking me, Seamus Fitzgerald, was fouling me so often that Joe Sherwood in the *Evening Press* said if it was a basketball game he'd have been sent off. With about a minute to go I got onto another ball and was cutting inside when I was hauled down by what Downey described as 'a rugby tackle'.

It was a free from the 21-yard line. Knock it over and we're level and the ref will blow it up and we're going to a replay. Joe Corcoran came over to take it. Joe had scored seven out of seven from frees that day. But this one was from the right of the posts. And we had two free-takers. Joe took them from the left-hand side and the centre, Seamus O'Dowd took them from the right. He had scored one free early in the first half. So I came over to Joe and told him it wasn't his free to take, Seamus had to take it. So Seamus took it on, lined it up and hit it wide. Would

Joe have scored it? Probably yes, more than likely. He was far more experienced; he was pushing twenty-nine at the time. Seamus had captained the 1966 minors to the All-Ireland title just three years earlier so he was a young lad; the pressure of a last-minute free in a senior All-Ireland semi-final was a huge jump for him to have to make. But the arrangement was there for a reason. Both of them were right-footed. Corcoran wasn't as sure with frees from the right-hand side; O'Dowd was more confident with them from that side. Anyway, it wasn't to be. I think it had an awful effect on Seamus. It haunted him for a long time afterwards. Downey, in his match report, used a quote from William Allingham, the nineteenth-century poet and scholar, to capture poor old Seamie's plight. 'Oh, what a little thing to remember for years, to remember with tears.' Kerry went on to beat Offaly in the All-Ireland final.

But we were a coming team. In 1970 we won the National League, beating Down in the final. It was Mayo's first title in the competition since 1954. We had a power-ful spine down the middle from Ray Prendergast at full back to John Morley at centre half, P.J. Loftus and Joe Langan in midfield, John Gibbons on the forty, myself at full forward. J.J. Cribben, Joe Corcoran, Johnny Carey – there was a lot of top-class talent in that team.

A fortnight after winning the league, we beat Offaly in the 'Wembley at Whit' tournament. I scored four goals; unfortunately, two of them were disallowed! But I finished with 2–3 from play. For the previous eighteen months or so I'd been on a good scoring streak and in 1969, according to Owen McCann, broke the record for most goals in a single year. McCann was a prominent writer on Gaelic games and I have kept a piece at home that he did on the scoring statistics for '69. Apparently, I scored sixteen goals that year, including tournament games, which beat the record of thirteen, set by Paddy Doherty of Down in 1960 and equalled by Johnny Joyce of Dublin in 1962. Mind you, I didn't seem to have much time for the famous old GAA adage of 'Take your points, the goals will come.' I had goal on my mind all the time. According to McCann, I scored only seventeen points that year to go with the sixteen goals! My overall tally after thirty-seven games with Mayo was 20–24, an average of 2.27 points per match.

In 1971 a new and exciting awards scheme was inaugurated to honour the top fifteen hurlers and footballers in a given year. It was called the GAA All Stars and it was sponsored by Carroll's, the cigarette manufacturers. There was a bit of American razzmatazz about it all and it quickly became a really prestigious honour to receive. The players were chosen by a group of GAA journalists. I remember hearing through back channels that I was a strong contender for a slot in the full forward line. In fact, one insider who had sat in on all the meetings told me I was pencilled in for right corner forward. But then, at the eleventh hour, I was out and a fella from Antrim by the name of Andy McCallin was in. The full forward line that year was McCallin, the great Seán O'Neill and from Galway, Seamus Leydon. In '72 I was more or less in the same situation. Again, I was a live contender; again I got squeezed out. Paddy Moriarty from Armagh was chosen alongside O'Neill and Mickey Freyne from Roscommon.

With the '69 Connacht title and the 1970 national league under our belt, we were hot favourites to beat Roscommon in that year's provincial semi-final in Tuam. The Rossies had come into the game totally under the radar and boy did they make it count. We came into it cock of the walk and paid the price. According to Paddy Downey, Mayo were atrocious for most of the first half. 'It was quite astonishing,' he wrote, 'to witness the ineptitude of their efforts to play passable football.' We rallied in the third quarter and actually took the lead, 1–8 to 1–5, when John Gibbons scored a fine goal. But that was as good as it got. Roscommon took over again and went hard to the finish line. And that was Mayo in the 1970 championship done and dusted.

The following year boiled down to seven days in June. We got back to the National League final, which for some convoluted reason ended up being played at this time of year. Kerry beat us by three points and the following Sunday, Galway beat us by three in the Connacht semi-final.

Three months later I got an invitation to play with the Connemara Gaels in the New York championship. It led to a tangle with GAA bureaucracy which left a sour taste for a long time after. Mayo's season was long over by then and the Garda GAA club had no upcoming fixtures either. I conferred with Mick Connor, the club chairman, and he assured me I was good to go. This was a time when high-profile county players travelling to America was

becoming a trend. The clubs over there were getting generous financial support from the Irish business community;
there was plenty of cash floating around. The deal was
that they'd pay your airfare, put you up at no expense and
send you back to Ireland with a couple of hundred dollars
in an envelope for your troubles. And now I was being
invited onto this weekend gravy train. Three or four days
in New York, play a game, have a good time, come home
with a chunk of notes in your pocket? Sure, you couldn't
turn down an offer like that. Several other county men
were doing the same thing; in fact, there was one from
Galway, Tony Ryan, and another from Roscommon, Tom
Heneghan, on the flight out with me.

The match was in Gaelic Park. Connemara Gaels
were beaten by a couple of pints, then we all went off to
have dinner and a few pints. At one stage of the night, a
supporter who was the worse for wear came over and
asked me how much did I get for selling the game. What?
I was baffled, told him I didn't know what he was talking
about. So he informed me that I must have had money on
our team losing because I had chances to take scores but
had laid the ball off to other players who couldn't score.
This was despite the fact that I'd scored 2–1 from play.
Needless to say, I told him where to go and he took this
as his cue to start shouting abuse at me. Next thing he
was attacked by someone else who saw what was going
on and suddenly all hell broke loose. Seemingly there
were factions in the club and grievances among certain
members and it all came out in this eruption. The cops
from the local precinct in the Bronx had to be called

and they arrived in numbers to quell the melee. I wasn't having any hand, act or part in it until a fella swiped the night stick off one of the cops and tried to hit him with it. I grabbed yer man and a couple more cops piled in and brought him to order. A group of them were arrested and thrown into the police wagons and carted off to the station. I learned subsequently that they were released without charge only after the club paid a very substantial amount of money. That incident didn't put me off the experience one little bit. I made the same journey six or seven more times in the coming years, always enjoyed it and always came home with more readies than I went out with.

Back in Mayo a few weeks later I bumped into Fr Leo Morahan, the county board chairman. We fell into general chit chat. Fr Leo asked me what sort of form I was in football-wise, because I'd had trouble with knee cartilage and been involved in a car accident which left me a bit banged up. I told him I was grand; sure, wasn't I only back from New York where I'd played a game and scored two goals. He didn't pass much remarks about that. But the first week in October I received an official letter from the Mayo county board, signed by Fr Leo, telling me I'd been suspended from playing for making an 'illegal' trip and wouldn't be considered for selection for an upcoming game against Roscommon in the Gael Linn tournament. My offence was that I hadn't received official clearance from the county board and the GAA's central council. I didn't know I needed clearance from either of them. It was the first I'd ever heard of it. Once I established that my club and county teams had no fixtures to clash with it, I assumed I was free to travel. But Croke Park had seemingly introduced new rules and regulations to try and control this overseas traffic in players. The letter from the county board proposed to hold a disciplinary meeting on the matter and if I wished to say anything in mitigation I could do so there. The problem was that the meeting was scheduled for 11 October and I only received the letter a couple of days beforehand. With my work roster and everything, it was impossible for me to get down to Mayo for that meeting.

So I made it my business to travel to the Roscommon game and clear the air with Fr Leo there. I duly met him and told him that I knew nothing about needing clearance, and that I assumed if your club or county didn't have a fixture on the day in question, you could travel no problem. Morahan was a very strict, authoritarian kind of man. And his reply to me was that I needed to state my case in writing. But, I said, 'I'm telling you now what happened.' That was no good to him. He wanted it in writing. I was really vexed about that; he was being totally intransigent about it as far as I was concerned. So I decided not to bother my backside putting it in writing to him. My sense of grievance was compounded by the fact that three other Mayo players had travelled to New York a week after me and played a game in Gaelic Park. There wasn't a word about that.

There was a stalemate for months thereafter. Mayo played five national league games between October and Christmas of '71 but I wasn't involved. In the meantime, word leaked out that there was some sort of stand-off going on between me and the county board because I wasn't being picked and my name was conspicuous by its continuing absence from the team sheet. Donal Carroll from the *Evening Herald* got in touch with me in November and instead of hiding from the controversy, I told him the whole story. It was published in the *Herald* and my predicament generated a lot of sympathy among Mayo supporters. The general feeling was that the county board were making a mountain out of a molehill and keeping me out in the cold for no good reason. Basically, I think it was making the board look a bit silly. I'm sure it didn't make them feel very comfortable reading about it in a national newspaper. The heading was large and read 'Very Little Justice for Big Willie McGee'.

Anyway, a week or two later wasn't I patrolling down Grafton Street one day in full Garda uniform and there I was approached by a Fr Paddy Mahon from Galway, brother of Jack, the All-Ireland winning footballer. Fr Paddy was himself a high-profile figure in Galway GAA. I don't know how he did it, but he was looking for me and managed to find me walking down Grafton Street on this particular day. He'd been requested to look for me by his fellow man of the cloth, Fr Leo. He explained that Morahan had asked him to meet me and get the explanation from me in writing about my adventure in New York and why I hadn't sought official clearance. Naturally enough, I was taken aback by this approach out of the blue, and in the blue, on a public thoroughfare from a priest I hardly knew. But he was very keen to explain that this would only be a formality, an exercise in ticking boxes. Once I wrote the letter, I'd be cleared to play again. Reading between the lines, it was obvious to me that Morahan was backing down; he just needed a token concession from me so he could save face and get rid of this embarrassing situation.

I told Mahon I didn't have any writing materials on me. I'd have to go back to Pearse Street station to get it. He said it didn't matter, it could be written on anything, so long as he was able to go back to Fr Leo with something in writing. So, I had a brainwave. I had a box of Major cigarettes in my pocket! Would that do? This amused Fr Paddy greatly. He said it would. So I took out the fag box, removed the remaining fags, and flattened it out to pen my affidavit, as it were. I duly inscribed the words:

> *To Whom it Concerns,*
>
> *I wish to state I was totally unaware of my obligation to get permission from the Mayo county board and the Central Council before travelling to play a game in New York.*
>
> *Yours sincerely, Willie McGee.*

Or words to that effect. I signed it and handed it over to Fr Paddy and he went away, more than happy that he'd completed his task.

I never heard any more about it from Fr Leo. I have no idea if the note was ever entered into the files of the county board, or indeed what became of the Major cigarettes packet with its all-important letter on the back of it. Did Fr Leo actually bring it to a meeting of the board and register it formally in the correspondence? Or did he just discreetly let the whole matter drop? I've no idea. All I know is that when the national league resumed in February 1972, I was back on the team.

Again we got back to the National League final and again we were beaten by Kerry in Croke Park. In Connacht we had an almighty struggle with Sligo in the semi-final, only finally beating them after extra time in a replay. Roscommon put five goals past us in the final and that was us done for another year. A year later Galway racked up 1–17 against us in the final and we were gone again. In '74 they put up 3–11 against us in the semi-final, another season over.

We had Sligo in the Connacht final in Markievicz Park the following year. They missed a clear goal chance in the closing minutes and we missed one at the other end no more than sixty seconds later. Peter Byrne was there for *The Irish Times*. 'Willie McGee's adroit flick left J.P. Kean in the type of isolation that forwards only dream about. But with almost everybody in the ground prepared to acclaim a goal, Kean's shot hit the underside of the crossbar and was hustled to safety before the bemused Mayo forwards realised quite what was happening.' And we had two simple chances to kick the winning point after that as well but made a hames of them.

Sligo beat us by a point in the replay in Castlebar two weeks later. It was a famous win for them, their first Connacht championship since 1928 and a glorious moment for Mickey Kearins near the end of a great career.

I had a goal disallowed for being in the square, allegedly; and on another occasion, when I punched a ball in mid-air, it looked goal-bound too, only to be denied by the crossbar. I was also booked in that game, having never been booked before in my life! Sligo's John Brennan was a good, rugged full back, but I took exception when he came through me going for a low ball and gave me a knee in the back for my trouble. We had words and they weren't too kind. I swung a belt at him and though I missed by a good twelve inches, he went down on the floor like he'd been poleaxed by Sonny Liston. I've met loads of people over the years since who tell me they were there the day they saw me floor the Sligo player with a left hook. I keep telling them I missed him by a mile. The referee was standing close by and saw the incident. He knew I missed him, so I got off with a warning that I should not have swung at him at all.

There's another incident from that match; it can be seen on YouTube: a high ball drops in or around the large parallelogram; I rise and get a fist to it and it flies over the bar. I'm running back outfield when out of the blue, Barnes Murphy kicks the legs clean from under me, completely off the ball, and in front of the referee too! It was a clear sending-off offence, but of course that didn't happen. When my kids and their friends have watched it over the years, their first question is, 'Why didn't you hit him back? Why didn't you plaster him?' But Barnes was a Garda too and went on to have a very distinguished career in the force. And I think that's what held me back too. You couldn't have two members of An Garda Síochána going pell-mell at each other in front of 30,000 people in MacHale Park.

And it wasn't my style anyway. It wasn't really any Mayo player's style. The general consensus is that this was our problem down through the decades, or one of them at least. That we were never cynical enough on the field of play. There's something in it too. I mean, it was the law of the jungle back them times and it would remain that way until the GAA finally cleaned up its act in more recent years. But back then it was dog eat dog kind of stuff. I saw a lot of talented players getting kicked and punched and receiving no protection from referees or linesmen or umpires. The likes of Joe Corcoran, Mickey Kearins, Dermot Earley, to name but a few. The famous Galway three-in-a-row team of the '64, '65 and '66, they took no prisoners. They had a ruthless, cynical edge. Their trainer was the famous Tull Dunne and he had it driven into them – take no prisoners. We had nobody like that. We were always a bit naive. We didn't have it drilled into us to win at all costs. It was a case of go out and play the game the way it's meant to be played and the net effect was that we let the other team play too. Many a time we could have stopped a forward coming through if we'd been blatant enough about it, but we didn't, and it's one reason why we lost a lot of close games.

I wasn't to know it at the time, but the replay against Sligo in '75 would be my last championship match with Mayo. In the spring of '76 we were preparing for the first round of the championship against Leitrim. We were in the gym in St Muredach's College in Ballina throwing around a basketball. I went up for a high ball, got bumped on my way down and landed awkwardly on my ankle. The ligaments were badly torn and a piece of the bone came away too. For a finish, I needed three operations to get it fixed.

For months afterwards I hated the game. I wanted nothing to do with it ever again. But by the following year I got my appetite back and started running and cycling. I began playing with the Garda club again and soon enough my form came back. In fact, it wasn't too long before I was flying fit again. Then I got selected to play for an All-Ireland Garda selection against a combined universities team in Croke Park. I had a stormer of a game. Henry Gavin was playing with the varsities team that day. He was already a fine footballer with Mayo, and he came up to me afterwards and asked where had I been hiding? Was I interested in coming back? But I was married with children by then and I was wary about the time away from home it would require. Then my old teammate Johnny Carey came to me. Johnny had recently taken over as manager of the county team and he wanted me back. So I said yes. The lure of wearing the jersey again was too much to resist. I knew I was taking a risk with my reputation. When a player comes out of retirement, there's always the risk that he won't be the same as he was before and supporters are liable to blame him then if the team doesn't succeed. But I thought it was worth a shot. Mayo had a lot of young players coming through and maybe an experienced operator like myself would be able to make a difference. I had just turned thirty. In previous years, the likes of Paddy McCormack had come out of retirement for Offaly, Mick O'Dwyer for Kerry and Jimmy Keaveney for Dublin, so it could be done. It might work out.

Johnny was in the guards too and he well understood my difficulty with work rosters and travelling and all that. If I was working Sundays and had to take them off to play games, I'd be out of pocket regarding the Sunday allowance in my salary. I had a mortgage too by that time and my wife Elizabeth had quit her job to look after the children. Johnny said it was no problem; he'd go to the county board and get them to make up the difference in my work pay when needed. He explained the situation to Mick Higgins, the chairman. The answer was no. Johnny came back to me and told me that Higgins had said to him that McGee should be paying to wear the Mayo jersey, not looking for money to wear it. I was absolutely gobsmacked. Couldn't believe he actually said such a thing. I was very hurt by it. And needless to say, that buried my Mayo career for good.

It was a career that had started out so full of promise. I was sure I'd go on to win several provincial titles and get at least a couple of cracks at an All-Ireland final. But the 1970s were to be a lost decade for Mayo football; we wouldn't win Connacht again until 1981. Given that reality, a Connacht medal and National League title are something to be grateful for. And I had some brilliant experiences along the way between the games themselves, the travelling I got to do and the friendships I made. I had an awful lot of good times representing the county. I stayed connected in the decades after through the Friends of Mayo supporters club and was heavily involved with various fundraising enterprises and golf classics and the like. Like many more fans, I've travelled in hope to Croke Park over the last ten years, following the adventures of that wonderful Mayo team. I've learned to hide my disappointment after all the times they've come up short, but deep down you'd be feeling it in your bones.

The world has changed to an unbelievable degree since we were young bucks kicking a ball around Dick's Field in Newport. The feeling in my heart for the red and green jersey remains the same. I hope and pray that the players of today can bring us to the promised land. All I would say to the present generation of up and coming forwards is, raise the green flag as often as you can. Or to put it another way, take your goals, the points will come!

6

THE GHOST

In 1971, back in the day job, the Garda authorities set up a unit called the Crime Task Force (CTF). It was to be a mobile, fast-acting patrol unit that could roam across the city and respond quickly to any incident as it was happening. I applied to get on it because the work appealed to me and it could be a stepping stone to get into the Detective branch. I was interviewed. They could see I had an interest in tackling crime at the coal face and I was duly transferred to the CTF.

It was headed up by an inspector, had four or five sergeants and about fifteen Gardaí. We were still in uniform, but there were a few differences all the same. We drove around in unmarked cars, not your regulation blue Cortinas with all the official trappings. The car I spent most of my time in was a white Hillman Avenger. It made a big difference because you couldn't be easily identified. It was easier to do surveillance anonymously. You could arrive to a scene without standing out from the crowd and giving offenders a chance to do a runner, which they would do if they saw a marked blue Cortina coming their way. In fact, we were so stealthy in it that a few criminals took to calling the white Avenger 'The Ghost'. We ghosted in and ghosted out. We were allowed roam across the city without being earmarked for a given district at an appointed time and place. It was less structured that way. You could go where the action was; some particular districts were hot spots and we could turn up there and give them our focus for a week or two before moving on again. We didn't have to work crazy hours of the day and night and we were able to make a few extra bob through the subsistence allowance if you were away from your station for days at a time.

In July 1972 we were in The Ghost on a patrol going up Ormond Quay when I came across another man who got very nervous when I jumped out of the car and approached him. He had no need to be nervous at all because I approached him looking for his autograph. His name was Al 'Blue' Lewis and it wasn't hard to pick out a tall, broad black man in Dublin at the time. I recognised him straightaway because of my lifelong love of boxing. Lewis was in town to fight Muhammad Ali. He looked every inch the trained heavyweight boxer that he was, 6'4" and I'd say a good 16 stone.

He instantly put his hands up when he saw me coming. He had done a long stretch in prison back in America. I shook his hand and said welcome to Ireland. I explained I was a huge fan of the sweet science and offered him my official notebook to sign. He was happy to do it and we got chatting for a few minutes. He said any time he'd ever been approached by police before, he was handcuffed and arrested. He thought the same was going to happen here.

He ended up inviting me to be his guest at the fight in Croke Park, but I thanked him and told him I had my ticket got already.

I went to see Ali training in the big handball alley at Croke Park that week too. Poor old 'Blue' was on his own that day on Ormond Quay. Ali was like the Pied Piper; he had huge crowds milling around after him; the place was packed with cameramen and reporters too. This was a public training session to generate more ticket sales, but Ali wasn't messing around. He went through a punishing workout of skipping and sparring and stomach beatings and all the rest. And I remember vividly when it was over, he was panting from the exertion. He'd been wearing this sort of heavy rainproof jacket which was tightly elasticated around the waist. It wasn't hanging loose on him. The elastic was folded snugly around his torso, so that when he was finished, he grabbed it and pulled it away from him and a gush of water fell out of it. He was shedding the pounds and he had spilled so much sweat that it gathered in a pool at the bottom of his jacket.

When another world heavyweight champion came to town, I made sure to meet him too. I think it was 1980. I found out that Floyd Patterson was on a visit to Ireland and staying in the North Strand Hotel. He was married to a woman from Offaly. I brought my eldest son David along to meet him too. A finer gentleman than Floyd Patterson you could not meet. I have a lovely photograph of the three of us together.

The late, great Jimmy Magee was a walking en-cyclopaedia on boxing and he had met them all during his days with RTÉ. And Jimmy would be the first to tell you he'd met them all! I got to know him over the years from all sorts of events and functions, but the first time I met him I was playing for a GAA selection against the famous Jimmy Magee All-Stars, his great charity fundraising roadshow. The match was in Clane in Kildare as far as I remember. Anyway, I might still have been playing for Mayo at the time, or I was recently enough retired from county football, so I was still flying fit and still thinking like a competitive footballer. Whatever happened, Jimmy was going for a ball and I lunged for it and I got in under him and turned him upside down. Sure, I didn't mean it at all. But Jimmy reared up on me and fucked me out of it. He got awful thick with me altogether. And that was my introduction to the bould Jimmy Magee! We got on like a house on fire after that, no bother at all.

Back on the job, we were floating around Portobello one day in the car when I saw a fella shuffling down South Richmond Street, wearing dark glasses and holding a white cane out in front of him. A blind man. I took another look at him. He was a big strong man in his forties. A bell went off in my head. We'd been circulated a day or two earlier with a physical description of a prisoner who'd broken parole. And he wasn't just any prisoner. Frank Murtagh had beaten two elderly ladies to death in their shop in Ballybough in 1964. The lady and her sister ran the shop. He attacked both of them; he beat them viciously with an iron bar; he robbed the till and ran. He was tracked down and sentenced to life in prison. But apparently, he'd been a model prisoner and was now out on temporary parole.

But he didn't return by his allotted curfew time and all garda stations in the city were duly notified. I'd never clapped eyes on him before, nor had I seen a photo of him. But, looking at this blind man on the street, I twigged something. If you got past the glasses and the cane, he answered to the description of the man on the run. I got out of the car, came up on him from behind, and just said, 'Frank.' He turned round straightaway and that was enough to confirm who he was. So was the fright on his face. He saw me well enough too. He knew immediately he was dealing with a guard. In fact, I wouldn't be surprised if he had 20/20 vision.

I told him who I was and that I was arresting him, and he immediately acquiesced. He just put his hands up and said, 'No violence.' I cuffed him, put him into the car and we deposited him back in Mountjoy prison. I can't remember what he did with the glasses and cane. On our way to the Joy, he told me he was worried about his mother. She'd be worried about him and he wanted to get word to her that he was back inside. So I made it my business to call to her home in Walkinstown and let her know the story. She too was an elderly lady, living on her own as I recall, and very shook by the circumstances her son was in. Obviously you couldn't ignore the irony of a man who'd been so concerned about his own mother being so cruel and violent to two other elderly ladies. But I had sympathy for his mother. It was a sad ordeal for her. She didn't have a car and she asked me if I could pick up a few messages for her in the shop. I said I could and I did. In the following months I'd call to her occasionally and bring her her bread and milk and whatever else she needed from the shop. And seemingly because of that, Frank had the height of time for me. He took to ringing the station from the prisoners' phone and telling me bits and pieces of gossip he picked up in jail about various crimes and criminals and all that. Sometimes he'd be right, sometimes he'd be wrong. He ended up ringing me so often that he became a nuisance.

He suffered from paranoia and nerves. He was a very fearful type of fella. For a man who had meted out such violence, he was afraid of his own shadow. That was why he'd meted it out to two old ladies, I suppose. He ended up severely institutionalised. He'd get out on parole from time to time but couldn't really cope outside the prison walls. Inside, he had the doctor when he needed the doctor and he had his meals every day and went to bed when he was told to go to bed. He was finally released in 1986 after thirty-two years, one of the longest-serving prisoners in the history of the State at the time. I never heard from him again.

But picking up Frank Murtagh that day on South Richmond Street was a major feather in my cap. He was the most wanted man in Ireland for that brief period when he was unlawfully at large. The longer he was missing, the more of an embarrassment it was for the prison authorities and the Gardaí. And God forbid, but what if he was to carry out a similar sort of attack again when he was on the lam? You'd be talking major questions for the Minister for Justice then. I got a letter of commendation from a Chief Super and that went into my file. I presume it helped when I applied to join the Detectives in the summer of '75.

7

FRAUD SQUAD

The word 'fraud' is used as a collective term for a number of statutory and common-law offences, there being no specific crime of fraud. The nearest crime relative to the word would be conspiracy to defraud. For investigative purposes, however, fraud is a very relevant term, constantly in use and very descriptive of the specific activities whereby an advantage is gained by unfair means, the advantage usually being of a pecuniary nature and by means of deceit.

Frauds are as varied as human ingenuity and imagination. Schemes to defraud are constantly being thought up and practised by professional fraudsters. The measure of their success is dependent on the extent of their victim's gullibility. Their essential weapons are a combination of confidence, false representation, pretences, deceits and omissions, all of which they use to exploit the greed, compassion, sympathy and trust of their victims. The successful fraudster must have considerable powers of imagination, when called upon, know how to tell lies well, have the ability to seize any opportunity that arises and above all must be able to inspire confidence.

Many criminologists consider that fraudsters have no superior intelligence but are endowed with a certain amount of trickery, deceit, cunning and hypocrisy. They depend on speed of thought, action and reaction to assist them in their misdeeds.

***

There was a senior detective, Sean Ryan, who had a saying that always stuck in my memory. He'd recite it almost like a verse from a poem when a new batch of fresh-faced guards would arrive to begin their careers in plain clothes.

'He's out there smiling, a young guard directing traffic while grim-faced detectives mingle with the crowd.' I'm not sure I fully knew what he meant, but I suppose it was something to do with the innocence of a rookie guard in uniform and the contrast with a serious-looking detective who was doing important business and had long ago lost his naivety.

They were a different breed of police man, the detectives, and in the Fraud Squad the first obvious difference was in the clothes they wore. The old-school investigator back in the '70s would often wear a three-piece suit with a handkerchief in the breast pocket and a trench coat for outdoors and a trilby hat. Kind of like what you'd see in the movies.

And that was one of the attractions for the likes of myself who had ambitions to become a police detective. There was a certain kind of glamour to it. You got to wear a good, well-fitting suit. The hairy old heavy uniform could be left hanging in your wardrobe. You'd have the freedom to put your hands in your pockets and walk around in your civvies without being conscious of everybody looking at you in the street. And in 1974, seven years after passing out of Templemore, I was buying a few good suits for my new job. I'd been interviewed by a couple of detective superintendents out of the Central Detective Unit (CDU) in Harcourt Square. The CDU encompassed all three national units of the Garda Síochána's detective force: the Serious Crime Squad, the Drugs Squad and the Fraud Squad.

I spent my first year with the detective unit in Pearse Street station. Then I was assigned to the Fraud Squad in Dublin Castle. My preference would have been the Serious Crime Squad, but you went where you were told to go – and that was where I was told to go. I knew nothing about fraud and you got no training in it either. You learned on the job; in at the deep end; watch and listen and learn. And I learned from two of the best men in the business. Detective Inspector Con Donoghue from Cork was the head of the squad at the time and he was a walking encyclopaedia on fraud. He had been involved in the famous investigation in the 1960s concerning the Shanahan Stamp Auctions company and the rare stamp dealer Paul Singer. It was basically a massive pyramid scheme that imploded in on itself and left hundreds of investors badly burned. In fact, that investigation ultimately ran for decades between all the court cases and appeals and the massive financial fallout from the affair. The late Detective Sergeant Matt Madigan from Dublin was another brilliant fraud investigator, I learned loads from him too.

And no doubt about it you had loads to learn. Investigating fraud as opposed to ordinary crime was a whole different ball game. It was slow-moving and complex and painstaking. You had to absorb an awful amount of intricate detail from reports, balance sheets, correspondence, all sorts of paperwork. Often it was written in legal or financial jargon. You would literally have hundreds of typed A4 sheets on your desk that you'd have to pore through and try and make sense of. You had to familiarise yourself with the Bankers' Book Evidence Act of 1879 and the subsequent amendments to it over the following eighty years or so.

Basically, you were operating a different part of your brain; you were operating in a totally different world to the one where you were dealing with belligerent drunks outside of a dance hall on a Saturday night. That was why a big majority of the police force wanted nothing to do with fraud. They'd run a mile from it. Most guards didn't get into the job to find themselves up to their oxters in paperwork. And that was why Fraud Squad personnel were kind of classified as a little bit above the detectives operating out of a police station, or the Special Branch man, or the lads in the Drugs Squad. These fellas didn't wear suits all the time; you didn't need to be wearing a suit when you were tracking down gougers or drug dealers or subversives. In the Fraud Squad you always wore a suit and some chaps would go the whole hog with a three-piece job, a handkerchief and a hat. You weren't going

into rough neighbourhoods trying to find criminals of
every description, you were going into banks and building
societies and offices and businesses. It was white collar
crime and you were a white collar detective.

* * *

In 1976 the banks were confronted with their third
workers' strike in ten years. In 1970 they were shut down
for over six months. This time the bank officials were out
for about nine weeks. And any time the banks weren't
functioning, the number of fraud cases shot up. To try
and keep trading, businesses big and small had to resort
to transactions largely done by cheque book. And with
the banks closed, there wasn't always a way of verifying
that there was money in the account to meet the cheque.
A great many transactions had to be done on trust and
sometimes when there is only trust involved, people
can be desperate enough or dishonest enough to chance
their arm and pay for something with a rickety cheque.
Several car dealers for example got stung. A lot of cheques
ultimately bounced. Customers bought new cars and the
dealers accepted the cheques as genuine only to find that
when the banks re-opened and they went to cash them,
they got hit by the cheque coming back off the crossbar. A
lot of dealerships went bankrupt as a result. A lot of small
businesses in general were wiped out.

As I was learning the ropes in those early days, I ended
up doing basic paperwork such as photocopying these
errant cheques and all the accompanying documentation

as business people tried to salvage some money by lodging complaints of fraud.

H Williams, the supermarket chain, also had a bit of sorting out to do over cheques and cash and the gap between the two. One solution was offered to them by a seemingly wealthy chap named Eric Maitland Woolf. We came to know him just as Maitland Woolf. Now, to look at him, you'd never have thought he was wealthy. He dressed like a down and out you'd see tramping the streets. He wore a long shabby coat, battered shoes and raggedy trousers. He was diminutive, not much more than five foot tall. He usually carried a bag with him, a cheap gym bag, but we never knew what was in the bag – probably piles of cash, as it turned out. I doubt it was sports clothes. He looked like someone who didn't wash too often, never mind follow a fitness regime. But in fact, we were led to believe he owned a few houses in Rathmines. H Williams had a supermarket on the Upper Rathmines Road. So he'd have become a familiar figure to the managers in the supermarket over the years. And when the bank strike happened in '76, H Williams being a cash business had a different kind of problem. They had no bank to lodge their daily takings into. Apart from the bookkeeping inconvenience, it also presented them with a security problem. This was where Mr Woolf stepped in. He offered to take the cash off their hands, or a certain amount of it anyway, and issue a cheque for each sum in return. Now I assume he was charging them a fee for this service, some sort of percentage cut off each transaction. H Williams were happy enough to go along with it because despite his appearance, they knew he had a lot of money and property. They thought his cheques were as solid as the Bank of England.

Anyway, when the bank strike in '76 kicked off, Woolf was soon going into H Williams in Rathmines at closing time and coming out with bricks of cash stuffed in his gym bag. Maybe his pauper's appearance was a security measure of sorts, a disguise to hide the fact that he was walking around with so much money. A couple of gougers looking for an easy mark wouldn't have reckoned that a hobo was worth robbing.

Every couple of days, then, he'd take the boat to the Isle of Man. He had a bank account in the Isle of Man for years, probably a string of them. Being a British citizen, it would have been straightforward for him to open bank accounts there. He'd lodge the cash there and come back to Dublin and repeat the exercise. When the bank strike finished in September '76, H Williams lodged the cheques, but they came back from the bank with the words 'refer to drawer' attached. Because each time he wrote a cheque, there was enough money in the account to meet it at the time. But by the time H Williams went to cash the cheque, several weeks later when the banks re-opened, Woolf had transferred the money from that account to another account. He had multiple banks accounts in Dublin.

It was basically a form of what they call circular kiting, or teeming and lading, whereby the player keeps moving money between his accounts, keeping one step ahead of the cheques as they arrive to be cleared. It's like a game of musical chairs in a way. He exploits the time lag between the cheque being issued and the cheque being cleared and during a bank strike this time lag went from your normal three days to weeks and then months. Part of Woolf's scheme was to make sure that when he issued a cheque to H Williams for a given amount of cash, there was enough money in the relevant account to meet that cheque at that particular time. This was enough to cover his ass when we came after him because the legislation around fraud was so weak and so full of holes at the time.

When the music stopped playing, H Williams was left high and dry for tens of thousands of pounds. And most of it was in Woolf's accounts in the Isle of Man. But we didn't have the legal powers to open up his accounts in the Isle of Man; we had no jurisdiction there. There was no money-laundering legislation in Ireland at the time either. And he was also smart enough to keep his lodgements just under the threshold permitted by law back then for the transfer of money from one jurisdiction to another. If the limit was £10,000, he'd be lodging £9,999. He was a very shrewd, strategic operator. Needless to say, no one in the relevant bank or banks in the Isle of Man asked too many questions either. He'd built up a personal relationship with them, just as he'd done with the staff in the Dublin Savings Bank over a period of years. It didn't matter that he was a peculiar, eccentric sort of chap. Maybe he was just one of those wealthy people who look as if they live like misers. Mr Woolf was bringing in loads of cash every week, and that was all they needed to know.

Eventually, when the manure hit the fan, H Williams senior management came to us looking to get their money back and to see Woolf put away for fraud. The hole it left in their finances was so big it nearly brought the company down. They were in a state of shock. They were angry and embarrassed at having been taken in hook, line and sinker by this strange creature who'd led them on a merry dance. These were men in suits who'd have considered themselves to be big shots in the management game. And yet one girl working at one of their checkout tills would've been able to take one look at Woolf and tell them straightaway that he was a dodgy article.

We took a load of statements from the supermarket managers, went to the banks where Woolf kept his accounts and tried to join the dots in this maze of lodgements and withdrawals. The paper trail was unbelievably convoluted and complicated. We put together a profile on Woolf, put all the evidence in a file and sent it off to the office of the Director of Public Prosecutions (DPP). Eventually, and to the surprise of nobody in the Fraud Squad, a letter came back from the DPP saying 'No Prosecution'. We knew this was going to be the result. It was definitely a fraud, but you couldn't prove his intention to defraud and that was the kernel of the whole investigation.

Technically, legally, he would be able to plead his innocence under the legislation of the time. It was so weak that he was able to pull off this massive swindle while technically staying on the right side of the line. The fraud legislation had so many gaps and loopholes, it was basically just one big hole held together with the paper it was written on. He was able to do enough to keep himself one step ahead of the law, even when the law caught up with him. And along with that, our paper trail hit a stone wall once the money crossed the Irish Sea. Our paper trail ended at the port in Dun Laoghaire. Woolf knew what he was doing from the first move on the chess board to the last. He knew that in the washout, all the cheques wouldn't be honoured, the missing money would be in the Isle of Man and he'd have covered his tracks.

H Williams went bust in 1987. As for Maitland Woolf, when he wasn't swindling supermarkets or duping bank tellers this self-proclaimed academic and book-lover continued his intellectual pursuits, which also apparently included philosophy, as well as antiquities, astrology and the occult. In 1978 he was elected chairman of the Philosophical Association of Ireland at their AGM. He died in 1990 and was cremated at the Glasnevin Crematorium.

8

CONNING THE CONMAN

The Bank of Ireland (BOI) has a branch in the village of Taghmon, about ten miles west of Wexford town. In 1979 it was scammed out of 25,000 punts, which is roughly €125,000 in today's money. It was a brilliantly organised con job. The only fly in the ointment for the ringleader came when one of his associates tried to swindle him out of £2,000 of the stolen money.

One day the branch in Taghmon found their phone lines acting funny. Then they got a call from someone purporting to be a senior technician with Telecom Éireann. This chap told the bank official that they were having technical problems in the area but were doing their best to fix them. He also said that if the branch experienced further interruptions in the coming days, not to worry, Telecom were just conducting tests as part of their investigations into the problem. The bank official said fine and no one suspected anything.

About a week later the branch got another call from the same 'Telecom technician'. He was just ringing them as a courtesy to say that the phone lines would be going down for the next half hour or so, depending on how long it took them to conduct their tests. Again, the bank said fine; everything was tickety-boo. This of course was in the days before mobile phones and caller ID systems and the like.

In the meantime, on the same day in Dublin, five men were preparing to enter five different branches of the Bank of Ireland. Their visits would be choreographed, staggered at roughly six-minute intervals successively. Each man was carrying a forged bank draft worth £5,000 Irish pounds. The drafts were themselves genuine in that they'd been printed by the Jefferson Smurfit company in Bray as authorised by BOI. These drafts would have had the security features of the time embedded in them. They were official monetary instruments. The only problem was that these drafts had been stolen from the Smurfit print works. The criminal in question had then filled in the blanks: the sum of £5,000 made out in the fictitious name of each of his five bag men, and issued on the Bank of Ireland in Taghmon. The bag man would present himself at the counter of his nominated Dublin branch looking to cash the draft. He would offer a forged document such as a driving licence as proof of identity. He would say he had an account with BOI in Taghmon in Wexford. The teller would then take the draft to his or her supervisor, who in turn would phone the branch manager in Taghmon to confirm the identity of the customer in question.

And this was where the Telecom Éireann part of the deception came into play. The ringleader or a few associates in his criminal circle had the engineering ability to divert the phone line and re-route it to another location where the ringleader would be waiting on the end of the line. One by one the bag men entered their assigned branches in Dublin, and one by one the calls started coming through to this fella waiting in a shed. He was now impersonating the manager of the branch in Taghmon. Let's say the first fraudster's name was Mick Murphy. The relevant bank official in Dublin would ask his Taghmon counterpart if he knew the payee in question, Mick Murphy. And yer man would reply, 'Oh yes, I know Mick Murphy well. He's banked with us for years. I can vouch for him.' And he could give a physical description of Mick Murphy too, if that helped reassure his caller further.

The ruse worked like clockwork. One by one the bag men entered a branch in Dublin and one by one they came out with 5,000 Irish pounds in cash. After the fifth accomplice completed his task, the conspirators operating the ad hoc telephone exchange restored the line to the branch in Taghmon. The ringleader, posing once more as the helpful chap from Telecom, then rang the actual manager, told him the problem was sorted and apologised for the interruption to the phone service. The manager thanked him for his help and that was the end of this minor inconvenience as far as he was concerned. The criminals must have had a good laugh among themselves over how perfectly they had suckered the poor unsuspecting manager in his office.

The penny only dropped two or three days later when the drafts came back to Taghmon for clearance and they were discovered to be forgeries. Then they started piecing the chain of events together. The Fraud Squad was called in. When we got a handle on the complexity of the operation, we soon enough reckoned there was only one gangster operating out of the south-east who would have the planning ability and logistical capacity to pull it off. It was a weasel we'd had dealings with before, a member of Saor Éire who was involved that same year in a foot and mouth extortion attempt that I deal with later. We put a surveillance operation on him and his associates and compiled a large dossier on them but couldn't unearth the telling evidence to effect an arrest.

But about two weeks after the fraud was perpetrated, a call was put through to me at my desk in Dublin Castle. A male caller was on the line. He would not give his name and he was muffling his voice to cover his tracks. He said he wanted to speak to somebody involved in the investigation into the recent Bank of Ireland fraud. I told him I was one of the investigators. He said he had information on one of the five bag men. The caller said that this fella had taken the money from a branch of BOI in Thomas Street, Dublin 8. It was obvious now that the caller wasn't bullshitting me entirely because I knew that Thomas Street was one of the five branches that had been robbed. But very few other people outside of the investigation would have known that. Next thing, he told me the fella's name and the place where we'd be able to find him – a mews at the back of a certain property in Fitzwilliam Street, Dublin 2. He hung up. I immediately alerted some colleagues and we went about applying for a search warrant for this property. Apart from questioning the named suspect, we hoped we might find some of the bank drafts that were still unaccounted for from the batch stolen out of Smurfits.

Once we got the warrant, probably the next day, myself and Det. Sgt Gerry O'Connor and Det. Garda Mick Maguire made a beeline for the address in this posh part of town. We knocked on the front door. After a delay we heard the sound of someone shuffling down the hallway. But he didn't open the door. A male voice asked who was calling. We identified ourselves. There was a long pause on the other side of the door. After several more seconds and no sign of the door being opened, I dashed around to the rear and lo and behold, there was a man, a fella in his twenties, squeezing himself out through a window at the back of the mews. But it was a small window and he was relatively rotund and he was struggling to squeeze himself through. He was red in the face and obviously panic-stricken. He got an awful land when he saw me, especially when I let out a few shouts at him. I can't remember what I said, but it must have been along the lines of 'What the hell are you doing?' I grabbed a hold of him and pushed him back in the window he was trying to come out of. Then I followed him in the window. Being skinny was a help here. Yer man inside was totally cowed; he was shaking like a leaf. He didn't give me any bother. I escorted him to the front door and opened it for my colleagues. We ordered him to give us a tour of his rooms. The search turned up nothing in the line of bank drafts or any other incriminating documentation.

We arrested him and brought him for questioning to

Harcourt Terrace station. The man is still alive. He went on to have a very successful career in the entertainment industry. For the purposes of this story, we'll call him John. John cried like a baby in Harcourt Terrace. He nearly had a nervous breakdown. He confessed everything. He told us about his part in the plot and he identified the ringleader; it was the same guy who'd been on the phone to me; the guy out of Saor Éire. He said he would admit to everything concerning his part in the conspiracy, but he would not, under any circumstances, identify the ringleader in his evidence. Basically, he was terrified of the man in question; he knew that this fella was dangerous and he wasn't wrong there. It was frustrating for us because we understood that John had been a pawn in the operation; the fella we really needed to nail was the guy in charge. We promised John we'd guarantee his safety if he did go on the record, but he wouldn't budge.

One thing we did establish was why the Saor Éire psycho had shopped John to the police. It was because John had tried to be far too smart for his own good. He didn't know who he was dealing with. John had gone to university and thought he was a lot smarter than he actually was; he was arrogant and naive. Not alone was he willing to break the law, but he decided to try and con the conman who'd put the whole fraud together. He was way out of his depth here.

He had spun a web of lies to the ringleader. John told him that the bank manager in Thomas Street had refused to cash the whole draft; he'd given John £3,000 and would only give him the balance when the draft was cleared. It was a cock-and-bull story and our Saor Éire patriot knew it. And being the cold-blooded type that he was, he actually rang the manager of the branch in Dublin 8, told him he was a member of the Fraud Squad investigating the robbery and that he needed to establish the exact amount taken from the branch. He was so plausible that the manager fell for it. The manager told him that he'd handed over the full amount £5,000. John's goose was cooked after that. When he refused to hand over the remaining two grand, Mr Saor Éire got on the phone to the Fraud Squad and ratted on him to me. The conductor of the orchestra wanted his pound of flesh. It would give you a good idea of how vindictive he could be, because by ratting on one of the gang, he was taking a big risk of exposing himself too. What if John decided to name and shame him in a court of law? But that was a risk he was prepared to take to get revenge on someone who'd swindled him. When members of a gang turn on each other, it can get very vicious between them. Maybe that's why John would not give up this guy's name on the record. The ringleader was part of an organisation that had murdered Garda Richard Fallon in 1970 and was known to be ruthless when it came to violence and robbing banks and the like.

John's case went to court and he pleaded guilty to the crime of obtaining £5,000 on foot of a forged instrument. But his family paid back the money in full, his solicitor said he came from a good background, had no previous convictions and would never be in trouble with the law again. John's solicitor also portrayed him as an innocent victim who was down on his luck and had been manipulated by a professional fraudster. We were not in a position to tell the judge about John conning the conman, which could really have swung the outcome of the case. It was the only time in all my years investigating fraud where I came across the conman being conned by one of his lackeys. But we couldn't get into all that in court because we'd have needed to name the leader and John would not co-operate on that score. The defence would dismiss it as hearsay. The judge marked the conviction as proved and gave him the benefit of the Probation Act.

As far as Mr Saor Éire was concerned, we hadn't the legislation back then, nor the wherewithal, to follow the money trail to get into his bank accounts and see if we could trace the money. The legislation around fraud at the time was so weak that we were investigating him with one arm tied behind our backs, if not two. We didn't have enough evidence to bring him in for questioning and even if we did, we knew that we might as well be talking to the wall. He had been arrested by Special Branch numerous times before for different things and he wouldn't open his mouth. He'd pick a spot on the wall and stare at it. All he'd do was smile and sing dumb. We had no fingerprints, no bank drafts, no phone calls traced – it would have been a pointless exercise. It would have made a lot of us very happy to get him into the dock but we didn't.

He had a number of prior convictions to his name, but only a few of us got to see just how sinister he was. For example, when he was living in St Mullins in Carlow, there was an elderly widowed lady living nearby. He wanted to buy land off her; she didn't want to sell. So eventually he intimidated her into selling. One night a window at the front of her house was smashed. The head was cut off a live chicken and the chicken was thrown through the window; it sprayed blood all over the floor and walls as it careered around the place before dying. The poor woman was absolutely shattered by the incident. Within a few days she was in her solicitor's office telling him to sell the land to this awful bastard who was terrorising her. The last I heard about him was when he died a number of years ago. He apparently died by poisoning; we don't know how he was poisoned or why or who did it, but that was the last we heard about him.

We still don't know how John ended up getting involved with this scumbag back in '79. Maybe they just came across each other in a Dublin pub; I have a memory that both of them drank in O'Donoghue's on Merrion Row. But Mr Saor Éire would have been looking for runners for that job and maybe John was badly stuck for cash and decided this would be a handy shortcut.

Within weeks of the court case, the manual file on John disappeared from the offices of the Fraud Squad. Just vanished into thin air. Almost certainly, someone inside was bribed to remove the file. The case was not reported in the newspapers at the time either, as far as I know. John got on with the rest of his life. For those of us who investigated him at the time, it didn't sit well to see him hailed as a pillar of society in the decades to come. We had a different take on him. And I still have a different take on him. He was a thief and a liar – and a leopard doesn't change his spots as far as I am concerned.

9

FOOT AND MOUTH

In late August of 1979 a letter landed on the desk of the private secretary of the Department of Agriculture and Fisheries. The anonymous writer demanded a ransom of £5 million from the State – roughly €27.25 million at today's rates. If the money was not forthcoming, he and his co-conspirators would unleash the Foot and Mouth virus on the State. It was an attempt at blackmail, at the extortion of a huge sum of money using the threat of biological warfare. We would discover during our investigation that among the plotters were a barrister, no less, and his associate, a former member of the Saor Éire terrorist splinter group – the same individual who had orchestrated the cheque fraud at the Taghmon branch of Bank of Ireland.

It was a one-page letter, typed. The Minister for Agriculture at the time was Jim Gibbons. I reproduce it here exactly as it was written at the time, mistakes and all:

*Dear Minister,**

to get straight to the point this is a demand
for £5,000,000. (five million pounds).

During the last four years, the writer and
four of his colleagues have considered sending
this communique to the Irish Government. We
have spent large sums of money researching
this idea. Several times we were almost ready to
to send this letter but the circumstances were
not right.

The reason for you paying us £5,000,000 is
very simple. If you do this we shall not introduce
to this country one of the most deadly and
costliest diseases that could aflict any country, in
particular an agricultural country, namely Foot
and mouth disease.

Let us assure you Minister that we have both
the facilities and determination to introduce this
disease if you do not pay our demands. However
at this stage we need not go into elaborate details
as to our ability to what we say.

We would like you to reply to us in the
Personal Column of the Irish Times on Saturday
September 1st. If you are prepared to consider
our requests, simply state in the reply; "Tom
Smith has read your message and will consider
your proposals", also state a reference number

---

* All the letters in this chapter are reproduced exactly as they were written,
with punctuation and spelling mistakes included.

*which we can use on uor next letter which you
will not recieve until December 1st.*

*If you do not insert the reply in the news-
papers we shall take it that you are not prepared
to no matter what the consequences. In this case
we shall communicate further with you. But we
will immediately take steps to introduce the disease. If you do reply please be prepared to. pay
uor demands because in our next letter we shall
prove without doubt our determination and
ability to carry out our threats.*

*Further if you do not reply, we shall, as soon
as cattle begin to go down, send copies of this
letter to all national newspapers.*

Trusting you will reply.

Unsigned.

The General Secretary of the Department of Agriculture
made immediate contact with his opposite number
in the Department of Justice who notified the Garda
Commissioner, whose office immediately called in the
Garda Fraud Squad. At this stage I had been a Detective
Garda for just over four years in the fraud division, based
in Dublin Castle. At about lunchtime on 29 August, I was
detailed to head over to the Department of Agriculture on
Kildare Street, to pick up some documents. There I would
meet a deputy secretary in the department. It turned out
that the documents were this ransom letter, a covering
note that 'Unsigned' had also written, plus their envelopes.
I went from there to the Garda Depot in the Phoenix Park

where I handed them over to the Chief Superintendent of the Crime and Security branch. He read the contents, handed them back and instructed me and Detective Sergeant Matt Madigan to interview the deputy secretary later that day. So, we met with him and an assistant head of the department's veterinary section. He told us that foot and mouth could most likely be deliberately spread here by introducing it into the animal food chain via the organs of an infected animal imported from abroad. For example, the tongues of infected beasts could be frozen and transported and thrown to pigs.

The first I ever heard of the Foot and Mouth disease was in December 1967 when reports from the UK informed us of the destruction of millions of cattle there as a result of the disease. The Republic of Ireland authorities were fearful that the disease would spread south through Northern Ireland, jeopardising one of the strongest industries here. The government decided to take action to prevent any spread and deployed a member of the Gardaí on every unapproved road leading across the border. They duly transferred members of the force from all over Ireland, myself included, to garda stations straddling the border. Having completed a month's tour of duty I was totally familiar with the prospective damage which could be caused in this country if we were hit by the dreadful Foot and Mouth disease.

As we discovered around the world in 2001, the foot and mouth virus can wreak havoc with countries and economies. It is highly contagious among cattle, sheep, pigs and goats. It can spread through one animal inhaling viral spores from its infected neighbour. We were also told that the conspirators might have been able to source foot and mouth bacteria from a vaccine plant in the UK or elsewhere.

This was an unprecedented criminal scam in Ireland. We had to take it seriously and for now we would have to play along with the mysterious criminals. The first step would be to place the ad in the newspaper Personal Column as instructed by 'Unsigned'. Even this wasn't a straightforward procedure.

On 31 August I went down to the *Irish Times* offices on D'Olier Street to place the ad. I spoke to the advertising manager and she said it would be fine, pending editorial approval. I paid in cash, collected the receipt and walked away. By the time I got back to the office, I discovered that the *Irish Times* editor had phoned and spoken to one of our senior officers. He wanted to verify that the Gardaí had indeed authorised this ad. In return, we asked that an exception be made to the newspaper's normal administrative procedures when taking ads: we did not want any record kept by *The Irish Times* of the person who was inserting the ad (me) or the organisation that was paying for it. Both sides were worried that the criminals in question might have a mole, a contact, somewhere among the newspaper staff. We were also worried that there might be a mole in Garda HQ in the Phoenix Park who would get their hands on this correspondence and leak it to the press. It would have been acutely embarrassing if this happened, not to mention potentially dangerous, because if the extortionists did have the capacity to inflict foot and mouth on the country, how would they react if they saw headlines about it in the national press? There were a lot of angles to consider in this unfolding scenario.

For the sake of continuity, and the consistent custody of all documents, I would be the middleman, between the Fraud Squad, the Department of Agriculture and *The Irish Times*. If and when the department got another letter from the conspirators, I would collect it and deliver it to the Garda inspector in charge of fingerprints at headquarters who in turn would pass it onto the handwriting experts. The letters would usually be contained in an envelope within an outer envelope. Once the outer envelope was opened to reveal the second envelope inside, addressed to the Minister of the Department of Agriculture or the Private Secretary of the Department, we were to be contacted immediately by a senior civil servant there. We established a working protocol around this documentation: the inside letter would not be opened in Kildare Street and indeed should be handled as minimally as possible. I would be sent round to collect the documentation and bring it back to our HQ. I would also be the officer designated to place each ad in the newspaper as demanded.

And as demanded, the first ad duly appeared in *The Irish Times* the next day, 1 September. 'Tom Smith has read your message and will consider your proposals.' We also included a reference number as requested: T.S. 300/79. Then we had to wait for them to make their next move.

On 29 November the next letter arrived. It was addressed to the Private Secretary of the Department of Agriculture. Interestingly, the envelope was date stamped

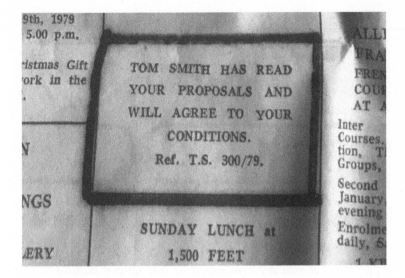

TOM SMITH HAS READ YOUR PROPOSALS AND WILL AGREE TO YOUR CONDITIONS. Ref. T.S. 300/79.

SUNDAY LUNCH at 1,500 FEET

'Ceatharlach – 28.XI.1979'. It had been posted from Carlow. Why Carlow?

Your ref. T.S. 300/79

Dear Minister,

Thank you for your reply in the Irish Times, Saturday 1st. September 1979. We trust you will continue to co operate with us.

Let us state from the start that we are totally determined to go through with our threats to spread this disease. During the last three months we have formulated the final details of our method introducing this disease. Your Veterinary advisors will have or can tell you, if you have not already been advised of the ease with which this disease can be spread. You and your entire department are totally helpless to stop us. We have selected a number of locations to which we have access and will use these outlets if we have to, but sincerely hope we do not have to do so, as we have no wish to see the Livestock industry totally ruined.

Now, Minister, let us talk about ourselves. We are five individuals with total different backgrounds and are each reasonably financially secure. We have expended quite large sums of money, both on travel and 'inducements' abroad to put us in the position we are now. We realise that if you are convinced of our determination to do what we say and you decide to pay the money to prevent this happening, one of your concerns would be that we would come back for more at some future date. We have no way to prove to you that this will not happen, but each of us will have recieved the sum of £1 million and this we assure you is totally adequate for each of us.

The ball is now in your court and you must decde what you must do, but bear a few facts in mind in making your decision.

No.1. There is no way you can stop us carrying out our threats.

No.2. Should you agree to pay the money, please be prepared to carry out the agreement as only one of the five will collect the money and this person will have no knowledge of the locations from which the disease will be spread.

If he is apprehended there is no way in which he can help you as he will not know these locations.

No.3. Our messanger is quiet prepared [for] the risk of being apprehended when he collects the money. Are you prepared to risk apprehending him? The decision is yours.

You will have received this letter by the end of November. On Saturday the 8th December we would like you to reply to us, once again through the Personal Column in the Irish Times. If you agree to pay the money you will simply state 'Tom Smith has read your proposals and will agree to your conditions'. You will then recieve a letter early in January giving you details of how the money is to be paid.

However should this notice not appear as requested we will assume that you are not prepared to meet our demands and we shall then prepare to carry out our plans in due course.

Trusting this will not be necessary.

Yours sincerely.

As they said, the ball was back in our court. We were beginning to get some sort of a psychological profile on the gang, or at least on 'Unsigned', and it seemed to us that this was an intelligent, thoughtful, strategic person. Spelling mistakes apart – and these could have been down to his flaws as a typist – he came across as highly literate and probably well educated. But beyond that, we didn't have much to go on. The Garda Document Section checked for fingerprints, indentations in the paper, the kind of envelopes used, the typing paper, the typewriters they were using and the kind of typeface on the page. Our fingerprint experts turned up various fingerprints, but none of them were identifiable in any way. They noted the typing errors in the text, which indicated that the letters were not typed by a professional secretary.

I went back down to D'Olier Street and booked another ad, to appear as instructed in the newspaper on 8 December. 'Tom Smith has read your proposals and will agree to your conditions.' Underneath the message we added the reference number.

Things started to pick up pace now. Ten days later, on 18 December, Agriculture received another letter from the gang. This time it had a Dublin postmark. And in it they were demanding that the money be paid in the following quantities and denominations: £2 million in German deutschmarks; £2 million in Swiss francs; £1 million in Irish pounds. All the money 'should be packed into one leather case'. They also asked that a diplomatic passport be issued and that a car, a white Mini 1000 with customised accessories, be used for the handover of the cash. And all of this was to be arranged by early January. Again, they asked that another ad be placed in *The Irish Times*, on 22 December: 'Tom Smith has read your message and has agreed to your proposals.'

But we couldn't continue with this carry-on. We had to make some sort of move. We had to try and put a bit of pressure back on them. So the top brass in the Gardaí and Agriculture came up with a different formula of words

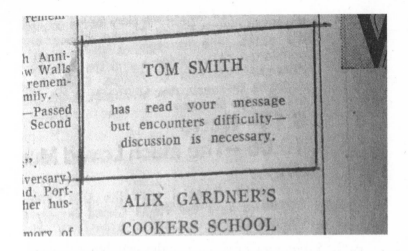

for the ad, to try to rattle them and flush them out from the cover of their secret letters. This time 'Tom Smith' wouldn't fully be playing ball with them. The wording in the ad on 22 December would read: 'TOM SMITH has read your message but encounters difficulty – discussion is necessary.' I went back down to D'Olier Street, gave them the wording, and it was duly published that Saturday.

Earlier that month, Jack Lynch had stepped down as Taoiseach and leader of Fianna Fáil. Charlie Haughey took over in both capacities and reshuffled the Cabinet. Ray MacSharry was appointed the new Minister for Agriculture. As I recall, neither Gibbons nor MacSharry became directly involved in the operational process around this case.

The different wording in the ad had the desired effect. The next day, a male caller rang the Department of Agriculture and asked for the Minister's private secretary. But it was a Sunday; there was no one around bar a few telephonists and skeleton staff. So the caller left a message: 'Tom Smith, 300/79, will telephone at 3 p.m. Monday afternoon: very important.' The caller was told that Monday was Christmas Eve and nobody would be working that day. He became very agitated and warned the switchboard operator to make sure that there would be somebody there on Monday to take the call. The Minister's private secretary at the time was a man called Cassidy. He was immediately contacted at home; it was decided that he and two colleagues would be in the office when the call came and that the call would be recorded.

At 2.55 p.m. on Christmas Eve the switchboard operator in Agriculture saw an incoming call on the board. She heard three distinct pips, which indicated an international or UK call. She answered; a female voice with broken English spoke and asked the operator to hold for a call. The female then put the caller through to the operator. A male voice spoke and asked to be put through to the Minister's private secretary. The conversation went as follows.

Male (M): Do you know anything about a notice in the *Irish Times*?

Cassidy (C): I can't hear you.

M: Repeat above. What is the difficulty, please?

C: Who's speaking?

M: Sorry, go ahead.

C: Are you the writer of the letters?

M: Yes.

C: I'll tell you why I'm asking you. You see we had three of them and two of them were in a different format to the third. Did you write all three?

M: The third was on a different typewriter, correct.

C: Oh, and you see as well as that we weren't expecting another letter until January, because that's what one of the letters said. I'm only identifying what you know.

M: I know what I'm doing, yes.

C: That [we] know that you are the person.

M: Can you be brief, please.

C: Yes, you see our main difficulty, well we have two difficulties but the main one is the diplomatic passport.

M: I thought so, that's all right, you can erase that.

C: In other words, no passport?

M: It doesn't matter.

C: Okay. Well, the second difficulty, I think we can overcome this one, is the car. There is a lot of trouble and a very awkward arrangement, but look here we might manage that one alright. But the main thing is the currency then. See, this foreign currency creates a problem for us.

M: Not very much of a problem I should think.

C: Well, it does because you see the – with the new EMS [European Monetary System] currency controls, the German marks are going to be a devil to get.

M: Well, we have plenty of time.

C: But you said in your letter early January.

M: We can wait if necessary.

C: Yes, and another thing, with all the denominations you mentioned of the three groups, including the small Irish notes, there is going to be a hell of a load of currency to cart around.

M: That's why I wanted them in Swiss francs and German marks.

C: Yes, but you also asked in Irish currency, do you know that.

M: What's your extension number and your name?

C: My extension is 5 here. (There's an interruption on the line and a series of bleeps.) Did you cut me off?

M: No, I'm calling from a phone box.

C: The name is Cassidy, the Minister's private secretary.

M: Very well, Mr Cassidy, I will be in touch with you early in January.

C: Early in January – well look, 5 is the extension at this room, but it's through that sub exchange you got through just now.

M: Right, goodbye.

C: Goodbye.

Christmas passed, the calendar turned to 1980 and on 15 January, the next letter arrived. This time they had a name to address. The writer began in courteous fashion.

> *Dear Mr Cassidy,*
>
> *Thank you for your reply in the Irish Times Sat 22 Dec. last. Also, for remaining in your office on Christmas Eve to take my telephone call.*
>
> *Our requirements remain basically as we outlined in our last letter to you. However we are prepared to go along with you when you say you are encountering difficulties producing a diplomatic passport.*

This is the only point [on which] we are prepared to give way. You are therefore required to comply exactly with each item we outlined in our last letter.

[He repeats here their demand for the money to be broken up in the various denominations, as per the exchange rate of 31 January.]

The entire is to be packed into one leather case.

The car is to be prepared exactly as instructed. On Sat. Feb 2nd 1980 the prepared car is to be parked for our inspection in the set down bay in front of The Gresham Hotel. It is to be parked there from 11am until 4pm. The case you intend using is to be placed on the front passenger seat. The driver is not to remain in the car.

The money is to be ready by end of Feb, by which time you will receive our instructions for delivering same.

As you are no doubt aware your request for discussions obliged one of us flying to London after your notice appeared in the paper. We are also certain you attempted to trace the call. We therefore do not intend having any further vocal communication with you.

As this stage we feel sure you are convinced of determination and ability to do as we have outlined in our previous letters. So, please do exactly as we have requested you.

Please reply in the Irish Times (Sat. 19th Jan)

> *stating you have received this letter and your*
> *willingness to comply with our requirements.*
>   *Tom Smith*

We duly placed the ad on 19 Jan: 'TOM SMITH has read your proposals and will agree to your conditions.' And we did agree to them, insofar as we decided to place the car outside the Gresham on the appointed date to see who might turn up. But the car in itself was going to be a challenge. They had outlined in their letter of 18 December their very specific requirements. It had to be a white Mini 1000. And it had to have a specific reg. number, REK 456 F, to be fitted to the rear, just above the number plate. It would also have to have two extra lights which would 'come on in conjunction with the normal brake and parking lights'. And on each side of the car a six-inch strip of reflective tape would have to be fitted, orange in colour. 'The tape is to run from front to rear wheels, the top of the tape being level with top of wheel arches.' As it happened, one of our colleagues had a brother with a white Mini 1000 and he agreed to have it customised as required. We went to a luggage shop to buy a suitable leather case.

With the car finalised, we prepared for the operation on 2 February. Coincidentally or not, this was the day of a rugby international, a Five Nations match between Ireland and Scotland in Lansdowne Road. (Ireland won with tries from Moss Keane and Terry Kennedy; Ollie Campbell scored 14 points.) Dublin was buzzing with crowds that day. I had the loan of my sister's Mayo-registered Mini; another friend also supplied his Mini, which we fitted with false plates. We parked the three cars in a row outside the Gresham, tight to each other, with the gang's Mini in the middle. The idea was that anyone checking it out would have to get up close to establish which one was theirs by locating the REK reg. plate. It would hopefully give a chance for our surveillance unit to get a good look at him. We placed the leather case in the passenger seat as demanded. We arranged for the local traffic Gardaí to put a parking ticket on each car after about half an hour because it would be abnormal for cars parked illegally in such a busy, prominent location to be left unticketed. We also had to tell the tow truck operators, who would usually be called on to remove cars causing such a blatant obstruction, not to take them away.

Detectives from the Fraud Squad with long lens cameras and video cameras settled in early for the stakeout. Some had secured the best vantage points in the county council offices across the road. Others were discreetly positioned in the foyer inside the Gresham. I was in the Eircom offices at the corner of Cathal Brugha Street and O'Connell Street with my cameras. It was a wet, rainy day. Passers-by stopped and chatted, smoked and lingered in front of the cars, blissfully unaware that they were all being secretly watched and assessed as potential suspects.

Nothing of note happened until, would you believe it, a detective chief superintendent from Garda HQ turned up at the scene. He was one of the very few outside our unit who knew that this stakeout was happening. But he was not part of the team. He just decided apparently to turn up and have a mosey around the parked cars himself.

We were furious with him. He could have blown the operation. If any of the suspects recognised him, they would have scarpered straightaway. No one could fathom why he turned up just like that and started hovering around the car in question. Of course, nobody had the bottle to question him about it afterwards, but someone should have. Anyhow, he disappeared and the operation continued.

Eventually, and to my astonishment, a barrister I recognised walked along the footpath, stopped at the Minis, sussed out the middle one, leaned over and took a close look at the reg. number. He walked around it to inspect the accessories – the luminous stripes on the sides, the two extra lights. I yelped out his name in surprise. 'That's yer man from the Four Courts!' I exclaimed. 'He's a barrister, a junior counsel.' But none of my colleagues knew him. I zoomed the video in on him to make sure we got good, clear footage of his face. But at the same time, I couldn't believe that this man of the law, this officer of the court, would have any involvement good, bad or indifferent with an extortion attempt on the State. He wandered away after a couple of minutes; no other relevant activity was observed for the rest of the day. At 5 p.m. the cars were driven away along a pre-planned route. We were mindful that the gang might have a counter-surveillance operation running parallel to ours, so we had spotters along the route as the cars were taken away to see if they were being followed or observed. The Mini 1000 in question was brought back to the Department of Agriculture as planned, just in case somebody had the Department under observation. The other two were driven away by male and female Gardaí wearing civilian clothes and Ireland team supporters' scarves.

It was only at the debrief after our stakeout that we began to piece the clues together about this lawyer. When I mentioned his name, saying that he was the only person on the day who appeared to have shown any interest in the relevant Mini 1000 (apart from the Chief Super), some other detectives reported that this same chap was a regular visitor to the residence of a known subversive, our Saor Éire hero mentioned previously.

He was living in the village of St Mullins, on the Carlow–Wexford–Kilkenny border, at the time of this foot and mouth extortion attempt. Which brings us back to the letter sent by the gang to the Department of Agriculture on 29 November: it was postmarked in Carlow. This had alerted Garda investigators to the possibility that this man might be involved in the blackmail operation. His house was under frequent surveillance.

And now it emerged at this debrief that the barrister spotted outside the Gresham that day had been a regular visitor to this man's home in St Mullins. It was still hard to take in that a lawyer could be involved with this kind of criminal enterprise, and with a seriously bad article like this fella.

But another piece in the jigsaw emerged when Det. Sgt Madigan got a report back on the letters from an expert, an academic in UCD we sometimes commissioned to form a psychological profile based on the language used in anonymous correspondence. In this case the letters were all typed, not handwritten, so as I understand it, he would have been examining the vocabulary, syntax, grammar, spelling, etc., to assess the literacy levels of the writer in question. There would be clues in the text as to a person's background, education, age and geographical origin, if you knew how to look for them. I would have had dealings with the barrister in the courts over the years and found him to be a very courteous gentleman. Anyway, this expert's conclusion was that the writer of these letters was very well educated, almost certainly a university graduate. He also figured that the letter writer had probably gone to a so-called good school, a fee-paying boarding school maybe. And amazingly, he was also able to make an informed guess as to when our correspondent had gone to this good school – the years 1965–70, he reckoned. The academic obviously didn't know that we had this barrister on our radar, but his conclusions only reinforced our own suspicions. There was one other pointer in this regard too: *The Irish Times*. The letter-writer was a reader of the famous 'Paper of Record'. He was familiar with its Personal Columns. There weren't too many fellas out there who were threatening the State through the Personal Columns of *The Irish Times*. And if your ordinary working-class criminal ever decided to put pen to paper, and engage with servants of the State through the newspapers, he more than likely wouldn't have chosen *The Irish Times*. This was one fraud merchant who came from a different social class than the usual duckers and divers. What's more, he was playing for far bigger money, and threatening the people with an agricultural virus that most run-of-the-mill scam artists wouldn't even have heard of. It was a mixture of arrogance and greed and ambition that is not unknown among privileged, highly educated young men.

This particular chap certainly had questions to answer. But we had not near enough proof to make a move on him. For starters he could offer any sort of excuse for being outside the Gresham that day, up to and including that he was meeting friends for a day's socialising around the rugby match.

The Chief Super, who'd nearly made a balls of the surveillance operation, attended the debrief. My photographs of the barrister had been passed around at the meeting. The Chief Super then had the gall to question me as to why I'd taken photos of the barrister! He didn't do it in front of the others, mind you, but waited until he could get me in private. I was only a young detective at the time and didn't feel I could put up an argument with this eejit. But the Detective Super in charge of the Fraud Squad, Con O'Donoghue, was present and fair play to him, he stuck up for me when yer man questioned me. 'Because it was good detective work,' replied my Super to this fella. And that put a halt to his gallop.

A few days after our appointment at the Gresham, the next letter arrived to the Department. It was postmarked 6 February 1980. And in it they got to the crucial part of the plot, the climax of the conspiracy – the handover of the money.

Dear Mr Cassidy,
Thank you for displaying the car as requested

outside the Gresham Hotel on Saturday February 2nd.

You will receive one weeks notice of the date on which we require the money to be paid. On the date that we require the money to be paid at 4pm the prepared car will once again park outside the Gresham Hotel and remain there with the driver and money inside the car. At 4.20pm the car will and procced along O'Connell Street via College Green, James Street to Newlands Cross. It will then park on the lay-by at the entrance to the Dublin-Naas Dual carriage way. It will remain there until exactly 5pm. At 5pm it will proceed in the direction of Naas and continue through Naas, Kilcullan, Athy, Castlecomer, Kilkenny, Waterford, New Ross, Enniscorthy, Arklow, Wicklow, Bray and finally back to Dublin. It will be necessary for the car to maintain a regular speed of 45m.p.h. on the open road and observe the speed limits in built up areas. It is imperative that the car does not exceed 45 m.p.h. but nevertheless travels as close as possible to this speed. Since the Mini will not have sufficient fuel to complete the round trip it will be necessary to carry 2-10 Litre containers of fuel to avoid having to stop at a garage to re-fuel. The car will stop as it approaches the bridge at New Ross and the driver will re-fill the cars tank from his two containers. It will be necessary for the driver to make adequate provision in order to

*avoid having to stop en route to either eat or go
to the toilet.*

*The car may not be fitted with any radio
transmitting or receiving equipment and if
this instruction is not carried out we will call
off the arrangements since it is easy to detect
such equipment. Needless to say there shall be
no attempt by Police or Special Branch officers
to follow the car containing the money or an
attempt made to intercept the pick-up Vechile.*

*In the event of these instructions not been
carried out and it becoming obvious to us that
the Mini is being tailed then the arrangement
will be called off. If we are forced to do this
you will receive seven days notice to have
deposited the sum of £10 million in a bank in
a foreign country that has neither sympathy nor
extradition agreement with Ireland.*

*If at the end of the seven days the money has
not been deposited we will then carry out our
threat and send copies of all our letters to you,
to the national newspapers. We trust this will
not be necessary.*

*Please reply in the Irish Times on Saturday
Febuary 9th acknowledging reciept of this letter
and accepting our proposals.*

Yours,

TOM SMITH.

There was an awful lot to talk about. The letter was so

packed with detailed, logistical plans, it would take a lot of time to try and figure out their strategy. Why did they choose this particular route: Dublin to New Ross via Waterford and back to Dublin again via Enniscorthy and Arklow? Where were they going to try and intercept the car? At the bridge in New Ross as our driver refuelled the car? That seemed an obvious opportunity. It would be the one time the car was stopped. But then again, they'd know that we'd have planned for this and prepared an operation to seize them on the bridge. The 45mph speed limit – what was that about? So they could synchronise the timing to make their move in their preferred location, at the precise time that fitted with their plan of escape once they'd captured the money? There was an incredible amount of detail to process and we didn't have time on our side because they wanted a reply in *The Irish Times* just a couple of days later on 9 February.

So, we had to play for time. The ad we placed in the newspaper was not as they'd prescripted. It read: 'No driver here will undertake journey. Can we negotiate more reasonable arrangements[?] Tom Smith.' We were suggesting that no one from the Department of Agriculture would undertake such a dangerous mission, delivering a ransom of £5 million to what would probably be an armed gang. Obviously, they knew that the Gardaí had been called in long ago on this investigation. They knew that we would be supplying the driver, if there was to be one, and it wouldn't be some civil servant from the Department of Agriculture. But we were being deliberately disingenuous to try and buy a bit more time.

They weren't long getting back to us. The next letter arrived three days later.

Dear Mr Cassidy,

Thank you for your reply in the Irish Times Saturday 9th Feb.

We cannot and will not accept your sugges-tion of changing our instructions. If you really intend paying the money without attempting to discover our identity we can see no reason for failing to obtain a driver to undertake the route demanded. In fact we have observed yourself and see no reason why you could not drive the car.

Please let it be clear that we are totally deter-mined, at this stage to obtain the money. Let us point out that these correspondences have been going on since last September. [It was actually August.] By this time you should be convinced of our determination. We require the money to be paid before the 15th of March. You will re-ceive 7 days notice of when the money is to be paid.

If you refuse to comply with the instructions in our last letter we will start an outbreak of this disease immediately. So, we would like you to confirm in next Saturdays Irish Times (Feb 16th) that you can and will meet our demands as stated in our last letter. We are not prepared to negotiate or yield in anyway whatsoever.

TOM SMITH.

Unusually, on this occasion they did not give us the specific wording they wanted in the ad. So we continued to play with the idea that this would be a high-risk undertaking for the delivery driver who would be the point of contact with the gang. Our ad read as follows: 'PREPARED TO CONCLUDE CONTRACT Transporter concerned at risk in delivery. Please demonstrate goodwill for his reassurance TOM SMITH'.

Again, they were quick to reply. The next letter arrived three days later. And here they went into great detail about how the proposed handover of the money would take place.

> *Dear Mr Cassidy,*
>
> *Thank you for your reply in the Irish Times Saturday 16th Feb.*
>
> *We too, will be pleased to conclude this business as speedily as possible. We can assure you and your driver that we have no intention whatsoever of injuring or harming him in any way. The weapon which we have threatened you with, namely, spreading this disease is the only one which we intend using. However, if it becomes obvious to us that we are being walked into a trap, we will simply call off the agreed arrangements and revert to what we stated in a previous letter.*
>
> *In order for us to carry out our plans it will be necessary for your driver to comply exactly with all our instructions. When we require your*

driver to stop a car will approach his car from behind. Our pick-up car will switch on and off its headlights 3 times (three times). It will then break to a halt with its headlights switched off. On this happening your driver will immediatly stop his car leaving the engine running and the headlights switched fully on. He will open the passenger door and dump the case from the front seat onto the grass verge on the left hand side of the road. He will immediatly close the passenger door and continue on his route given. He will still be observed for at least 30 minutes to give our driver time to complete its task. Under no circumstances is he to stop before these 30 minutes are up. After 30 minutes he is free from any given instructions.

Please bear in mind that while it is easy for you to arrange to have our pick-up driver captured and he will not even resist, we will still carry out our threat and spread this disease if he does not answer our telephone calls. He will be required to answer 4 (four) TIMED telephone calls at 4 different points. If he does not answer these calls, we shall, after making certain that he has been apprehended, start our plans to spread this disease. Please believe us when we say that our pick-up driver will know nothing of our plans for implementing this disease. He has not taken part in any of the arrangements, this had been deliberate. While he will be able to give you

*our identities it will be to late for you to stop us
and our letters to the press.*

    *We shall make no further threats to you nor
shall we attempt to use violence of any type to
get this money. The money shall be paid before
the 15th March in the manner requested.*

    *You will receive one weeks notice of when
we require the money to be paid and you will be
required to reply in the Irish Times to that letter.*
    TOM SMITH

By now senior officers were putting in place a major
operation to terminate this threat to the State, whether
or not the criminals actually had in their possession the
infected animal organs, or the bacteria, that would inflict
foot and mouth on the country. We could not at this stage
afford to take that risk. And we wanted to apprehend
them to finish this situation once and for all. It would
mean going along with their plans, *mar dhea*, getting a
driver, and organising a big back-up team who would
follow him as discreetly as possible. We did a dry run of
the route to and from Dublin that they'd instructed us to
take. We mapped the mileage between each town and the
time it would take driving at 45mph. On 1 March 1980
the Department of Agriculture received the eighth and last
letter from the gang.

    Dear Mr Cassidy,
    This is our final letter to you.
    We would like you to remain in your office

at Kildare St., from 3.45pm until 4.30pm on Saturday next 8th March. This is the date on which we require the money to be paid. The reason for this is so we can call off the arrangements if we foresee any difficulties. You have received in previous letters all our instructions, so please carry them out as outlined.

On Friday 7th March please confirm in the Irish Times that our arrangement stands.

TOM SMITH.

I headed back down to D'Olier Street one last time and placed the ad, which said simply that the arrangement stands. It duly appeared on Friday, 7 March. The next day was delivery day, D-Day. A massive undercover operation was about to begin. The code name for the operation was BLACK JACK. There would be around twenty-five detectives and Gardaí involved, including armed members of the Special Branch. The Fraud Squad was not an armed unit at the time. Many of the personnel did not know the background to this case; they were just there on the day to provide support. The Special Branch lads were just told in the briefing beforehand that it was an extortion case, that a cash ransom was being demanded, and there could be a shoot-out if the extortionists decided to hijack the Mini somewhere along the way.

Detective Garda Pat Walsh would drive the Mini 1000. The leather case was on the passenger seat, but there was no cash in it of any description – no deutschmarks, Swiss francs or Irish punts. It was stuffed, as I recall, with newspapers.

Pat, as instructed, would pull out from the Gresham Hotel at 4.20 p.m. We would have plain clothes detectives circulating around the hotel. A guard, casually dressed on an unmarked motorbike, would follow the Mini from an appropriate distance. He would follow until Rathcoole and head into Rathcoole garda station where he would join three other detectives in Car no. 1. Car no. 2 with three more members on board would be stationed in the car park of the Red Cow Hotel on the Naas Road. Car no. 3 would start from the Central Bank on Dame Street and follow the Mini to Newlands Cross. No. 4 would be on standby at Newlands Cross. No. 5 would take up the first surveillance phase of the journey when the Mini left Newlands Cross. No. 6 would be stationed near the Cement Roadstone plant outside of Naas. I was in this car. One by one we all pulled out, but there was no visible convoy. We were scattered here and there over a couple of miles behind the Mini. We stayed in touch on the car radios.

Meanwhile, the best guess by security chiefs was that the criminals' rendezvous with the Mini would take place not in New Ross but in Waterford, possibly on a bridge over the River Suir near the Waterford estuary. It was a plan that would make sense from the gang's point of view: intercept the Mini on a bridge, have the driver push the leather case out the passenger door, one of them would pick it up and hurl it over the bridge. Down below would be a speedboat; the criminals would pick up the case and take it out to sea via Waterford Port. And all done under the cover of darkness. In this scenario it could all happen very quickly. There would be no shoot-out and no car chase.

So, Garda headquarters contacted Irish navy officers and with them drew up a plan. Two of their vessels were mobilised, the LÉ *Emer* and LÉ *Fola*. Each of them had a Garda officer on board to formally arrest the suspects. Both vessels were present in Waterford harbour on the night. They had each lowered motorboats into the water in readiness to pursue the suspects' speedboat if necessary.

It turned out that it wasn't necessary. In fact, nothing happened at all. The Mini and its convoy of following cars made their way down through the designated towns, into Waterford and back to Dublin. There was no interception of the Mini, no pick-up vehicle flashing its lights three times, no final confrontation in this cat-and-mouse dance that had been going on for over six months. The only moment of alarm came somewhere near Arklow on our way home. Our car was the nearest one behind the Mini at this stage. Pat Walsh radioed us to say there was a car pulled in up ahead with its hazard lights flashing. He sounded worried and suddenly we were all on red alert. I had been issued with a handgun for the operation, as had the other members of the Fraud Squad. Mine was a Smith & Wesson snub nose 38 revolver. I took it out, in my panic thinking there was going to be a shoot-out and I was going to be like Clint Eastwood in *Dirty Harry*. But sure I wasn't used to handling a firearm at all. I got an unmerciful shake in my arm. I could hardly hold the bloody thing! It was trembling in my hand. Next thing we had gone by the broken-down car and Pat was telling us it was all a false alarm. Relax lads. Years later the Fraud Squad became an armed unit, I did my firearm training and actually ended up with very good results in the shooting tests. But I can tell you that the enemy would have been fairly safe from me that night in Arklow, if it had turned into the O.K. Corral.

And that, more or less, was that. So, unfortunately from the point of view of this story, there is no great climax to tell you about. But this is the reality of police work rather than the fiction of TV detective stories or Clint Eastwood movies. In those shows, there has to be a confrontation between the goodies and the baddies in the final reel, with the baddie getting his comeuppance. In our line of work it can consume a vast amount of our time, not to mention taxpayers' money, without any satisfying conclusion. Sometimes there's closure; often there isn't. And fortunately, from the point of view of the real world, no police man or woman was shot or killed on this operation; the State and its economy weren't damaged by a plague of foot and mouth; thankfully the whole thing ended with a whimper not a bang.

On the night in question, we all headed back to the Garda depot for a few drinks and to discuss the events of the day. We were tired and relieved. We weren't the only personnel involved to enjoy a few drinks that day. Word came back to us later that the sergeant assigned to one of the navy vessels wasn't exactly enamoured with the seafaring life. He'd been sailing and hanging around on board all day and his restlessness got the better of him. The ship was apparently well-stocked with duty-free whiskey and our hero decided to help himself to a stiffener – or ten! He'd have done well to make any arrests that night, by all accounts, if push came to shove.

We never heard from the conspirators again. They melted away like the snow. In due course the final reports on the case were drafted and filed, and we all moved on to other investigations big and small. The only suspect we had anything on was the barrister and it wasn't remotely enough. If it happened nowadays, he would have been arrested and questioned. But in 1980 there was no law in existence to cover an arrest of that nature. At that time we were operating under the Forgery Act of 1913 and the Larceny Act of 1916 which were very weak in terms of powers of arrest. We spent years trying to persuade the Law Reform Commission that the legislation relating to fraud badly needed to be overhauled. Eventually it happened with the Criminal Justice (Theft and Fraud Offences) Act of 2001.

And to be honest, even if there was sufficient legislation back in 1980, I think the powers that be at the time would have been very slow to arrest a barrister because of the all-round embarrassment and consternation it would have caused. It probably would have kicked off an almighty legal battle between him and the Gardaí and we wouldn't have had near enough hard evidence on our side to justify the time and money it would have cost. So, in short order, our friend got away with it. He went on to become a senior counsel, a member of the Bar Counsel and a member of the King's Inns Counsel. He got a lot of work from the State during the course of his prosperous career. He died in middle age.

10

CHEQUE MATE

There was a Garda colleague in the Special Branch who was fond of a punt on the dogs in Harold's Cross. Maybe too fond for his own good. He had an account with a bookmaker at the track and one day in 1988 he handed over his pay cheque to place a bet and get the rest back in cash. We were paid weekly in those days. This particular cheque was worth in excess of 600 Irish pounds. It'd been a bumper pay day for this officer because the normal weekly take-home pay would've been around £200. This one was obviously loaded with overtime and other allowances.

Anyway, the bookie passed on the cheque to another bookmaker for a lay-off on a gamble or some such other arrangement between them. This second bookie had friends in the criminal fraternity. About four days later bookie no. 2 handed the cheque back to bookie no. 1 who in due course lodged it to his own bank account. But for the few days it was in bookie no. 2's possession, it had ended up in the hands of a few career crooks.

All Garda pay cheques at the time were issued by the

office of the Paymaster General. The cheques were printed by a specialist printing company, but they had very few security features to protect them from forgery. They were printed in a plain, green and white colour scheme and didn't have the multiple colours or elaborate patterns that would have made them harder to forge. And it was this weakness in the system that the criminal ring in question exploited.

One of them was Fran 'the Lamb' Cunningham, a conman and fraudster of long standing. He was the older brother of gangsters John and Michael Cunningham who had received long prison sentences a few years earlier for the kidnapping of Jennifer Guinness. Fran 'the Lamb' often worked on various scams with other conmen, such as John Traynor and Seán 'Fixer' Fitzgerald, who feature in another chapter in this book.

Unbeknownst to us at this early stage of the conspiracy, the criminals had taken this one Garda pay cheque and gone to work on it. They blocked out the name of the payee and photocopied the cheque onto paper similar in weight and feel to the cheque, using a high-quality colour photocopier. They then took the copies and carefully typed in a fictitious name on the payee's line. They used the same name on every copy: 'Charlie Ryan', as I recall. Now they needed a front man, a fella to hand in these forged cheques over various counters and walk out with the cash.

Enter one Charlie Kirkwood. As far as we could tell, Kirkwood hadn't worked an honest day in his life. He was in his mid-fifties at this stage. He was never at the top of the criminal tree; he wasn't a headline act, but he was a perennial member of the loose alliance of crooks knocking around his part of the city. For the scam to work, they needed a fella who could pass himself off as a guard and they figured Kirkwood could pull it off.

This was despite the fact that he had a pronounced limp which made him easily identifiable to strangers, never mind guards. The story behind the limp was the source of much mirth. During a stay in Mountjoy many years earlier, he had tried to engineer an escape via the Mater Hospital. He feigned abdominal cramps or some such phantom ailment and got himself taken to the Mater. While there, he used the call of nature and got himself into a particular men's bathroom. This bathroom faced onto Eccles Street. The plan was to squeeze through a window and jump to freedom. Unfortunately, he overestimated his athletic ability. He would have to jump clear of the perimeter railing below to land on the street. And Charlie was no Bob Beamon. He landed on the railing, which sadly was topped by a row of spikes. Charlie ended up impaling himself on one of the spikes. According to the more lurid versions of the tale, it was his rectum that ended up impaled on the spike. He had to be delicately removed by medical personnel. At least they didn't have too far to go, and presumably Charlie didn't have too long to wait to be extricated from his ordeal. He was brought back inside the Mater; this time it was for real and this time his stay was much longer. The upshot of this escapade was that he ended up with one leg shorter than the other, hence the lifelong limp thereafter.

To play the part, Kirkwood and his cronies had to ready up a credible Garda ID card. They did a good job on that score. They procured a proper Garda shirt, Garda tie and Garda tie pin. We discovered afterwards they got these items from a serving Garda. This fella already had a dodgy reputation; he'd previously reported his ID card lost, not once but twice. You'd wonder where they ended up. Kirkwood also procured the official Garda wallet which housed your official Garda photo and name and rank and number. We think he got it from the same source. We couldn't prove it, but we suspected it was him, not least because he was subsequently seen in the company of various associates connected to the Kirkwood crew. This particular rotten apple was eventually fired from the force for other offences.

Kirkwood meanwhile presented himself at the main Dublin Bus office on O'Connell Street dressed in the light blue Garda shirt, replete with tie and tie pin. He wore a sports jacket over that. He got his photo taken here for the purposes, *mar dhea*, of getting himself a Dublin Bus pass. It would have been a head-and-shoulders picture, not full body length. Then he transferred that photo into the Garda wallet with the accompanying alias, Charlie Ryan, and forged Garda number to complete the impersonation.

The next step was to start cashing the phoney cheques. These were still the days before credit cards were widely used for ordinary transactions. People were still doing most of their daily transactions with cash. It was common enough for people to get their pay cheques cashed in pubs and shops. The bent cop who was liaising with the criminals was himself living in Rathmines at the time. He'd have known that a lot of guards based in that part of town would often get their cheques cashed in shops and supermarkets in the Rathmines/Rathgar/Terenure areas. It was money in the bank as far as these businesses were concerned. A Garda pay cheque was safe as houses. Most of the time the person behind the counter wouldn't bother verifying the identity of the guard handing over his cheque. There was so much deference in general to Gardaí, their cheques would be cashed without question.

Kirkwood started walking into shops in his Garda gear and walking out of them £600 richer every time. He would present the cheque and open up his ID wallet, but rarely, if ever, did the person behind the counter examine the ID closely. It just wasn't the done thing. And even if they did, his forged card was professional enough to pass muster. Various shopkeepers told us afterwards that because he was a man in his mid-fifties, it was another reason why they didn't ask to check his ID. It just didn't seem appropriate. They didn't want a scenario where they might be causing embarrassment to him or themselves by daring to question a veteran member of the force.

In due course, the bogey cheques started to emerge in the banking system. It wasn't too hard to spot them once they started rolling in – they all had the exact same serial number. And they all bore the name 'Charlie Ryan'. The conmen presumably decided to use the name Charlie on the off chance that if he was in a shop and someone came in who knew him and said 'Howya Charlie', he wouldn't be rumbled.

I was a detective sergeant in the Fraud Squad at the time, in charge of the stolen cheques and credit card section. Myself and my colleagues were put on the case. In the meantime, Kirkwood's scam was working so well that he expanded his operation to the banks too. He would hobble into various branches around Dublin with his cheques and hobble back out again with another £600 in his pocket. In fact, he was spotted by a detective in the queue in a bank in Clondalkin one day, but at this stage the scam hadn't been twigged.

With our investigation underway, we started taking evidence and eyewitness descriptions from the scammed shopkeepers. I circulated a notice to all garda stations about this ongoing forgery operation. It included a description of the suspect, with the significant detail that he had a pronounced limp.

On St Stephen's Day, Charlie got the wrong sort of Christmas present. He went into a small shop on the Upper Rathmines Road in his Garda clobber and once more tendered a dodgy cheque. There was an elderly lady behind the counter and she was so respectful of the Gardaí that she apologised profusely to the nice man for not having enough cash to make good on the cheque. In fact, she told us later that she felt sorry for this gentleman who was so urgently in need of money a day after Christmas. The banks were closed, he needed the cash and she wanted to do her best for him. She told him if he came back at three or four that afternoon, she'd have done enough business by then to be able to cash his cheque. Despite his cunning, Kirkwood was never the sharpest blade in the box. And he was dumb enough to sign the cheque and leave it with the lady. He told her he'd return later that afternoon.

Lo and behold, at some point in the interim, two actual guards sauntered into the shop looking to buy a few bits and pieces. This friendly, good-natured lady got chatting to them and happened to mention in passing that she was expecting their colleague back shortly to have his cheque cashed. Maybe it was playing on her mind, I don't know. But one thing led to another and she mentioned that the guard in question had a bad limp, the poor man. The penny dropped with our two fellas straightaway. They had seen the notice back in the station about the limping criminal and the forged cheques. They asked the lady to show them the cheque in question. They took one look at it and knew it was fraudulent. They returned to the station and told their story to their sergeant, Pat McGee (no relation), and a surveillance and arrest operation was scrambled together at short notice involving the guards in Rathmines station. They put their men in place, inside and outside the shop. Charlie duly returned later that afternoon. He was being driven around by one of the gang members. He was dropped off about a hundred yards from the shop; he hung back for a while to see if he could spot any sort of a trap; he didn't hang around too long; he wanted to get in and get out fairly lively. He was arrested in the shop. He was shocked when he saw what was happening. As he was being escorted out, he hurled a stream of expletives and obscenities at the poor old lady. She was badly rattled by the experience; she told us she didn't sleep for weeks after.

Kirkwood was formally charged in Rathmines station and transferred to the Bridewell for the night, pending an appearance in the District Court the next morning. Myself and a few others from the Fraud Squad were informed and attended in court that morning. He was remanded in custody for another week while the Fraud Squad took over the investigation. I eventually charged him on seventeen counts of fraud. We don't know how they divvied up the spoils, but the gang must have made off with over £10,000 in total before the game was up.

Kirkwood denied every charge, including even the last one pertaining to the episode on the Upper Rathmines Road where he'd been caught red-handed. So we had to organise an identification parade and these are not the easiest operations to conduct. In this case we had to find seven volunteers of similar age and height and weight to Kirkwood. If they looked very different to the suspect then his solicitor would kick up a fuss about it not being fairly set up. Your case could collapse in court over something like that.

The parade would be held in the Bridewell. We had to go into pubs and offices looking for volunteers who fitted our criteria and who would be willing to take part. Then we had to get all our witnesses from the various shops and banks he'd scammed. The witnesses had to be kept apart before the parade to make sure they didn't confer with each other. We lined up our row of men and Charlie could decide where he wanted to stand among them. Then we brought in our first witness and he scanned the row of faces. The witnesses had the choice of going over and putting a hand on the shoulder of the person they identified as a suspect or just pointing to him and stating where he was standing in the row of eight. The first and second witnesses identified Kirkwood more or less straightaway. Sixteen of the seventeen witnesses in total picked him out. Eventually we put the file together, the case was heard in the Circuit Court and Kirkwood was sentenced to six and a half years in jail. He was absolutely furious and so were his family members who were there to hear the verdict. There was an altercation outside the courts between them and a few other associates who'd been involved in the scam. Apparently, Kirkwood's loved ones felt he'd been thrown under the bus by these other latchicos – sure, what else did they expect? Six and a half years' jail was an exceptionally heavy sentence for fraud at the time. It was why they were so angry. Kirkwood appealed the severity of the sentence and in actual fact, it was lengthened in the appeals court to eight years! Needless to say, we were pleasantly surprised with that outcome.

But that was all in the future. Weeks after he was initially arrested, we received intelligence from a detective in Crumlin station that a similar forgery operation was about to go down, this time copying the pay cheques of prison officers. The detective had the full inside track on the plan. It was being engineered by our old friend, Fran 'the Lamb' Cunningham. Fran would be meeting an associate at the back of the Ashling Hotel, the well-known premises that stands near Heuston train station, at 1 p.m. on a particular day. We called in the National

Surveillance Unit to conduct the surveillance operation. I would stay well clear for fear of being spotted by a counter-surveillance procedure.

Fran duly met his man at the appointed time and place on Montpelier Hill. This fella was dressed up in prison officers' clothes. They made their way to Phibsboro, backtracking on their movements a number of times just in case they were being followed. They were being followed. We followed them to the Allied Irish Bank (AIB) branch in Phibsboro. They entered and joined two different queues. Cunningham went up to one counter and got a £20 note changed into coins, in the hope that this would provide him with an alibi if anything happened. The 'prison warden' went up to another counter, handed over the fraudulent pay cheque and got his cash. When they left, a member of the surveillance team approached the same teller and identified himself. He asked to look at the pay cheque and to his amazement saw it was made out to a 'Willie McGee, Prison Officer, Mountjoy Prison'. He got onto the walkie talkie straightaway to break the news. It was obvious that these fellas were taking the piss altogether. Not alone were they stealing money, they were trying to have a laugh at myself and the Fraud Squad too.

But for the moment, we didn't make a move. We tracked them as they repeated the same trick in the AIB in Capel Street and again in the AIB in O'Connell Street. After that, we decided to call a halt to the circus. They were arrested on Bachelors Walk on the way back to their car. But Cunningham was too cute and had been around too long to carry the can. It was the young fella impersonating the prison warden in the name of Willie McGee who ended up confessing to the whole crime after hours of questioning. He named Cunningham in his statement taken under caution as the principal conspirator. He was charged on counts of forgery and obtaining money using forged instruments. We prepared a file on Cunningham too, but the DPP decided not to run with the charges against him. The young fella had been released on his father's bail of £200 and disappeared. When we called to his father looking to find him, he told us off the record that the conspirators had given him the bail money on condition that the young fella never showed his face again. They warned him in no uncertain terms. The father advised him to head to London and that's what he did. And although he had implicated Cunningham wholesale in his statement, we needed him to give it as sworn evidence in court, otherwise it wasn't prima facie evidence. The prosecution was thwarted. The young lad had absconded and was never re-arrested or stood trial.

During our investigation we carried out a number of searches and located the seat of the crime. It was a flat in Rathmines; it had the typewriter used to enter the false names on the cheques; and it had the colour photocopier on which they were copied. They'd rented it from an office supplies company and we returned it to them.

As it turned out, our investigations into these scams led to us foiling a much more ambitious operation. Naturally we had taken in a few of Cunningham's cronies for questioning and were strongly thinking about charging one of them. He was very anxious to avoid an indictment and so he turned informer. He told us that the Garda and prison officer scams were trial runs for a massive fraud on army pay cheques. In fact, the money they creamed from the bogus Garda pay cheques was being used to finance this much larger operation. This one would be timed to coincide with a large contingent of Irish army personnel returning from their tour of duty with the United Nations in the Lebanon. Each returning soldier would be receiving a handsome pay cheque. The gang was planning to go to town on this opportunity.

The first part of the operation was to dispatch eight young volunteers in their twenties to Spain for a week of sunbathing. The ringleaders wanted these lads with tight haircuts to come back with a good tan, the better to impersonate a soldier who'd done six months in the heat of the Lebanon. Our informer knew when they'd be turning up at Dublin airport for their flight to Spain and we organised a heavy surveillance operation. They were photographed and videoed as they hung around in departures before boarding the airplane.

Meanwhile we alerted the Department of Defence and hatched a plan with them to reinforce the army pay cheques. In turn we liaised with the printing company. They had a specialist in security printing, Paul Delaney, and he came up with additional designs, including a sort of scratch card effect to be embossed on the cheques. Underneath the scratch area would be the word UNIFIL – the acronym for the United Nations Interim Force in

Lebanon. Following that, we gave warning notices to all the banks, building societies and major shops and supermarkets in the south Dublin, north Kildare areas. A majority of the returning personnel were living in those parts and it was our information that the criminals had targeted those businesses there. In fact, all the major financial institutions were notified by directive of the new-look army pay cheques.

The suspects came back to Dublin airport a week later and were filmed and photographed again looking suitably bronzed. The next step would be for these runners to start hitting the streets with their bogus pay cheques. But it never happened. A mole somewhere in the defence forces had got word back to the gang that the design of the army pay cheques had been altered. They knew straightaway they'd been rumbled. They knew that a police operation was underway and it spooked them completely. This massive fraud conspiracy was abandoned. I'd imagine Cunningham and his cronies were furious. They'd spent a lot of time and money in the planning and it had come to nought.

We arrested the eight runners and detained them for twelve hours each, but of course they denied any knowledge of any fraud conspiracy. They were just eight mates who'd gone to Spain for a week's holiday, even though they were all unemployed. We asked them where they got the money and they all chimed in with the same answer – they'd been saving for years. We heard afterwards that a few of them, maybe most of them, were happy and relieved that the conspiracy had been abandoned. They had enjoyed the holiday alright but were very nervous about having to do the crime.

* * *

My rather rocky relationship with Charlie Kirkwood had one more postscript three or four years after he was jailed. When I was a young detective in the Fraud Squad, his was a household name in the criminal underworld. He was famous for his skills ranging from forgery to logistics to safe-cracking. And he was notoriously elusive too; it was very difficult to pin him down on any charge. So it was a major feather in our caps to catch him and get him sent down for eight years.

After a number of years in the Joy he was let out on temporary release. He must have been pushing sixty at this stage but, evidently, he still hadn't learned his lesson. Once out of jail, he decided not to go back at all. So his profile was duly circulated in Garda bulletins – Mr Kirkwood was a wanted man again. Our paths had diverged since then and I hadn't heard that he was out on the lam until I got a call from the detective unit in Dundrum station early one morning. A bank manager had been kidnapped and a ransom had been demanded and paid. The detectives' investigations brought them to a public phone box in Bray. There they discovered a note left by one of the extortionists in the speaker of the phone. It was taken away for examination and fingerprints were found on the paper. They belonged to a fella based in Brittas Bay who I had convicted of fraud a few years earlier. At that time he'd been working as a car salesman and setting up false declarations on hire purchase agreements and skimming off commissions on both sides of the contracts. I'd investigated the case. He got twelve months in prison because he couldn't repay the money he'd stolen from the hire purchase company.

It was this prior connection that led to me receiving the call from the detectives. They had never heard of this guy. I got to Dundrum station as fast as I could. I had arrested this chap at his house in Brittas and knew exactly where to find him. While waiting for everyone to get organised I happened to pick up the station's 'routes'. These were the information sheets concerning crimes reported, people wanted on warrants, prisoners released, etc. And my eye fell on the name of Charlie Kirkwood. To my surprise I discovered that he'd broken parole and was out on the run.

We loaded up in cars and vans and made our way to the house in Brittas. The suspect was present and correct; he was stunned by this early morning call from the boys in blue. The house was searched from top to bottom.

The suspect remembered me from our previous engagement and we were actually having a civil conversation when I heard what I thought was a familiar voice coming from elsewhere in the house. Said I myself, that sounds a lot like Charlie Kirkwood. His name was fresh in my mind from reading the routes. I went down the landing to the source of the voice, which was now inside the bathroom. He was explaining to a detective standing at the bathroom door that he'd just been visiting his friend on an overnight stay from Northern Ireland. He had what sounded like a very convincing Northern accent too. He had handed over some form of ID to the detective which stated that his name was Charlie Byrne. So I stood outside the door and asked him to identify himself again. I could hear the tap running inside. He shouted out that he was Charlie Byrne and he repeated his story that he was just visiting from Northern Ireland and would soon be heading back there. But the more he talked the more I figured it was Kirkwood.

Out he came after a few minutes and I took a good look at him. The bit of hair he had left on his head had been dyed a sort of reddish ginger hue as part of his new disguise. But I knew exactly who it was. And I said to him, 'Good morning, Charlie.' If the first fella had been shocked by our arrival at this front door, it was nothing compared to Kirkwood's reaction now. He recognised me instantly and he went ballistic as I told the detectives to arrest him. He was shouting at me in his Dublin accent now. He was convinced that the whole operation had been a ploy to catch him, not the other fella. In fact, it had been a pure coincidence. None of the other officers knew who he was but I did, otherwise he might have blagged his way out of it and made good his escape.

We ended up walking out of that house with two wanted men, not one. The other guy subsequently admitted to playing a small part in the kidnapping of the bank manager. He wasn't really a hardened criminal; he was basically an amateur. He had left the note in the speaker of the phone in the public call box and had got a few quid for his trouble. I don't believe he knew how serious the full crime was going to be; he ended up getting five years in prison with two suspended. The main perpetrators were never found.

Kirkwood was ferried to Bray station that morning and taken back to the Joy from there to serve out the rest of his time. He died in February 2011 at the age of eighty. According to a short obituary in the *Evening Herald*, he'd been 'a well-known criminal in the capital since the 1960s. Kirkwood was pals with Seán "The Fixer" Fitzgerald, Martin "Viper" Foley and Veronica Guerin murder suspect John "The Coach" Traynor.' He had run 'a notorious betting ring called "The Toss School", which operated at Little Ship Street in the 1970s'. According to the report, a number of Dublin's longest-standing gangsters were expected to attend his funeral on Francis Street. I don't know whether they did or not because I wasn't there. And I didn't send flowers either.

11

WHITER THAN WHITE COLLAR CRIME

In a police officer's working life, he or she won't be expecting to come across servants of God breaking the laws of man. We have enough problems with ordinary civilians doing that, never mind men of the cloth or women of the religious orders.

I've come across two such cases, involving a nun and a priest, albeit that the woman in question turned out to be an impersonator and not a religious sister at all. She was rumbled when she stepped up to the counter of the bank in Dublin airport. My best recall is that it was some time in the late 1980s when I was a detective sergeant in charge of the stolen cheques/credit card fraud unit.

Anyway, we got a call one day from the branch in the airport telling us there'd been a female fraudster dressed in religious attire who'd tried to get a cheque cashed. But something hadn't sat right with the teller and he decided to ask the Mother Superior standing in front of him for some sort of identification. She said she didn't have any to hand

and as a nun it wasn't her practice to carry such ID with her. Obviously she was hoping that her special status would circumvent any need to prove who she was. But yer man still wasn't for budging and when he told her reluctantly that he was very sorry but he couldn't cash the cheque, the saintly facade wasn't long disappearing. All of a sudden, she turned into a swearing, screaming harpy. She unleashed a string of ferocious expletives at the teller before high-tailing it through the crowds and out of the terminal. She was long gone by the time we turned up at the airport. We took down all the details from the teller and one thing that always stuck in my mind was when we asked him why the alarm bell went off in his head when this holy apparition appeared in front of him. 'To be honest,' he said, 'I thought she was too good looking to be a nun.' In fairness, it was hard to keep a straight face after hearing that.

It must have been only a week or two later when the same lady fetched up again, this time in the west of Ireland. There's an order of nuns called the Little Sisters of the Poor; this one was intent on becoming a little sister of the rich. And the jewellery shops of Mayo were going to be her mark.

But she made a mistake. You'll find that fraudsters generally make a mistake somewhere along the line. The mistake she made was going into two jewellery shops near to each other in Castlebar. In the first one, she bought a number of items, including an expensive watch. She said she wanted a good watch to give as a gift to her parish priest. She signed the cheque and left. The owner discreetly came to his front door and watched her walking down the street and into the next jewellery shop. When she left that place, your man called in and asked about the customer they'd just served: the nun – did she by any chance buy an expensive watch and tell them it was for her parish priest? Indeed, she did.

Someone managed to catch the make of car she was driving and the number plate. They went straight down to Castlebar garda station and reported the matter. They reckoned she wasn't a nun at all and they were fairly certain that the cheques she'd just signed were bogey too. One bright spark in the station remembered that they'd got a notification about the episode in Dublin airport – someone masquerading as a nun going round with a stolen cheque book. Castlebar phoned the Fraud Squad and I took the call. The reg. number of the car suggested it wasn't locally bought; it might be a car-hire job, so I phoned Knock airport and talked to the car-hire people there. There wouldn't have been many other places in the vicinity where you could hire a car. Sure enough, she'd flown to Knock that morning, had hired the car there, all paid for by stolen cheques and facilitated by a forged driving licence. She was due to fly back that evening. The order was immediately given to local garda stations to track down this car. She was now a nun on the run, and this was like an Irish version of the movie *Sister Act*, with yer wan as Whoopi Goldberg tearing around Mayo with the cops on her trail.

I can't remember in what order she did it, but her whistle-stop tour took in jewellery shops in Sligo town, Ballina and Westport too. She was eventually stopped by Gardaí from Claremorris on her way back to Knock airport. Again, far from saying a decade of the rosary or two, the air turned blue when this lady of the veil was told she was going to be arrested. She turned vicious in fact, lashing out and making an awful scene.

I couldn't find any details of the subsequent court case online, but I remember that her name was Imelda and she had numerous previous convictions for cheque fraud and cashing stolen cheques. This was still the pre-computerised age. It was relatively straightforward to manipulate a stolen cheque book and cheque card. The original signature on the cheque card could be erased by soaking it in brake fluid, for example, and replaced by a forged signature on it and the cheques. The financial institutions hadn't got their security protocols in order; they left gaps in the process which specialist cheque fraudsters could exploit.

Sister Imelda was kept in custody and brought to Castlebar court, but the overall charges were dealt with in the Dublin District Court. She was treated leniently by the judge, as fraudsters usually were at the time, and served a short custodial sentence. The jewellery shops in Mayo and Sligo got their bling back and that was the last I heard of this fallen angel, surely the first nun in history to go to Knock without visiting the famous Marian shrine there. In my opinion it was no accident that she'd planned her robbing spree for Mayo. Having the airport there made it convenient from a logistical point of view, but she would also have hoped to be above suspicion down the country, where priests and nuns were still held in high esteem. The same level of deference might not apply in the city – it certainly had not applied in Dublin airport that day.

And it was the same kind of deference that an actual servant of the Catholic Church evidently exploited too when it suited him, a priest in rural Cork who wasn't shy about wielding his status in the community for less than godly reasons.

The first I heard of Fr James Davern was when I was superintendent in Macroom garda station. Upon promotion to the rank, I'd been transferred out of the Fraud Squad in August 1993 and sent down south, albeit that my family stayed in Leixlip and I commuted back home at weekends.

It was a different kind of police work down here, I can tell you. One of the cases I had to deal with concerned a shotgun being fired at the windows of a public house because the publican had put up the price of the pint by a penny. The government budget had hiked the price of alcohol, but the disgruntled customer in question reckoned that the publican had put the penny on stock he'd purchased before the budget increase and that it should only have applied when the next batch of kegs arrived. Another one concerned a farmer complaining about large stones being littered around a meadow of his, which would totally ruin his mowing machine when cutting the grass.

Anyway, I was in my office one day when I got a call from the chief superintendent in Bandon, Martin McQuinn. It concerned a priest in Ballinspittle, the village that had become famous in the 1980s for its moving statue of the Blessed Virgin Mary. His name was Fr Davern and he had been involved in a road traffic accident which caused serious injury to one of the passengers in the other car. Gardaí at the scene saw that his car had two bald tyres and because someone had been injured in the collision, the car would have to be impounded and inspected. He was cautioned that he might be prosecuted for a charge of careless driving. The car was taken to Bandon station where the Public Service Vehicle Garda inspector was based. This incident happened on the Friday of a bank holiday weekend and on the Sunday, Davern decided to pay a visit to the home of the superintendent of the Bandon district, Noel O'Sullivan. He wasn't in at that time, but his wife was suitably hospitable to a visiting priest and welcomed him inside. When Noel arrived home, he found this priest whom he didn't know sipping tea and chatting away to his wife. Soon enough, the real reason for his visit became apparent. Father wanted a discreet word with the superintendent. He was wondering if the little matter of the bald tyres could be finessed away; it was only a minor issue in the grander scheme. And maybe the careless driving thing could be … maybe … you know yourself. And he was also wondering if he might just be able to get his car back that very same day too. O'Sullivan was not impressed with this situation. Here was a stranger turning up uninvited to his family home on a bank holiday weekend and asking him to bend the rules and give back a car that had been involved in a serious accident. He politely told the priest it couldn't be done and ushered him out the door.

On Tuesday the car was examined by the PSV inspector

and Davern was phoned to come and collect it. He duly turned up, was given the keys and told to have the defective tyres replaced immediately. He left the station, but ten minutes later he was back. He walked into the public office and announced that he wanted to report a crime. There was £10,000 in cash missing. It had been in a plastic bag under the driver's seat when the guards impounded the car. The money belonged to the parish and it was gone. Basically, he was alleging that the money had been stolen from the car whilst it was in Bandon station, which was tantamount to saying it had been stolen by Gardaí. His statement was taken down and he left the station. The statement was immediately forwarded to Noel O'Sullivan. The chief super was duly notified and it was quickly decided that O'Sullivan could not investigate the matter because of the conversation he'd had at his home with Davern a few days earlier. The allegation was so serious that the Garda Commissioner's office was contacted for direction in how to deal with it. They decided that the case should be investigated by Gardaí from outside the Bandon division. Which was how I ended up getting the phone call from Martin McQuinn that day.

My first move was to get this fella into my office in Macroom and see what sort of an article we were dealing with. I phoned him at his parochial house and told him I'd need to take a full statement from him in person. He turned up on the agreed date in white collar and black suit. To my amazement, he had brought a solicitor along with him. You don't bring a solicitor along with you when you're making a statement to the police about a crime in which you've been the victim. Once inside my office I asked him why he had brought a solicitor with him. He said he wanted to have him there because he wasn't used to having any involvement with the Gardaí, which I found out later was a blatant lie.

I had a fair idea already that the story of the missing ten grand was a blatant lie too; it just didn't add up, it didn't make any sense at all. So I proceeded to give him a hard time in my line of questioning. What was he doing with ten thousand pounds cash in his car? Where did he get it? Why hadn't he lodged it in the bank? Was it in ten-pound notes, or twenties or fifties or hundreds? What kind of a bag was it in? Where did he get the bag? When did he put it in the car? Why didn't he take it out of the car before the Gardaí impounded it? Why didn't he mention it to Superintendent O'Sullivan when he called to his house on the Sunday? Why didn't he contact the Gardaí in Bandon about it?

He had come in to the station twenty minutes earlier very cool and confident in himself. But all of a sudden, he was tying himself up in knots with the answers he was giving. He was losing his composure – getting very hot under the collar, you could say. I think he was surprised that I wasn't treating him with the deference he was used to as a priest. I think he just assumed that because it was the word of a priest, it would be taken without question. 'Yes Father, no Father, three bags full Father.' But that day was gone, or it was going at any rate.

He went from surprise to shock when I raised my voice and put it to him that there was never any money in the car. It was a cock and bull story. He was making it all up. If the money was there, he should have gone into Bandon to collect it rather than calling to a superintendent's home and trying to pervert the course of justice. He was accusing Gardaí of stealing a large sum of money, which was a very serious allegation to be making in any circumstances. And he was wasting police time, which was an offence in itself too. He was badly rattled at this stage. And then, the solicitor interjected. He wanted a word with me in private. We left the room and he told me he wanted to withdraw from the case there and then; he no longer wished to act on behalf of his client. I asked him why. 'I'm sure you can read between the lines,' he replied.

We went back inside, the solicitor informed his client of his decision and departed. There was a heavy silence in the air now. Davern was stewing in his seat. I then asked him if he wanted to proceed with making a formal statement of complaint about the missing money. He said he would need twenty-four hours to think about it and that he would revert to me afterwards. I gave him my contact numbers and he left my office. The meeting had lasted less than half an hour.

He never got back to me and I wasn't one bit surprised. But I wasn't going to leave it lying there. I couldn't get him on the phone for several days. I left messages for him and eventually he got back to me. He said he was withdrawing his claim. I requested him to put it in writing. He promised he would but never did. I wrote follow-up letters asking him to put it in writing that he had withdrawn his claim. I didn't hear back from him, but it didn't make any difference to me – I was going to proceed with the charges against him anyway. I put the file together and submitted it to the Director of Public Prosecutions. I recommended that he should be prosecuted for wasting Garda time and for making a false complaint, an offence compounded by the fact that it had been levelled against serving members of the force.

In due course the recommendation came back from the DPP: no prosecution. I was annoyed and so were the relevant officers in Bandon garda station. They had this stain on their character hanging over them, made by a crooked priest abusing his power who had demonstrably made a false complaint and wasted Garda time. And yet the DPP didn't want to do anything about it. It's my opinion that the DPP's office was swayed by the fact that he was a priest; they recoiled from the prospect of a man of the cloth being prosecuted in court. It fell to me to inform Davern of the DPP's decision. Again, it proved very difficult to track him down. The bishop had him transferred to a parish in Cork city in the meantime, no doubt having heard about the carry-on and knowing full well about his troublesome attitude in general. When I tracked him down to tell him the news, he was able to tell me before I could tell him. He'd heard it already from somebody else. The Church wouldn't lack for friends and contacts in the legal system. Davern sounded very pleased with himself and made a point of telling me that the case should never have gone ahead in the first place; he was glad that someone had seen sense and called the whole thing off.

He didn't get away entirely scot-free. He was summonsed for careless driving and having two bald tyres in relation to the road traffic accident. He was arrogant enough not to bother turning up in court on the day of the hearing and in fact a warrant should have been issued for his arrest for failing to appear. But the District Court judge wasn't inclined to make this decision, on the grounds that Fr Davern might be busy with parish work on the day in question. The case was put back. Davern turned up at the next sitting where he was fined £250 and severely cautioned by the judge. But he wasn't banned from driving for a period of time whereas another ordinary civilian might well have been put off the road.

In the autumn of '94 I was transferred back to the Fraud Squad in Dublin. And that was where I had my next encounter with the same man in black. It was about three years after I returned. My secretary rang through one day to say there was a priest on the line. He was insisting on talking to the head of the Fraud Squad and no one else. So I took the call and he introduced himself: Fr James Davern from Cork. I sat up fairly straight in my seat when I heard that. I recognised the voice and the accent straightaway. But I didn't tell him who I was; all he knew was he was talking to somebody high up and that was what his ego wanted. So I let him fire away. His complaint concerned a solicitor who'd represented him in a claim for damages against Cork Corporation. He'd had an unfortunate run-in with a loose manhole cover on the city streets and as a result of the injuries sustained, he'd sued the Corporation and had been awarded a sum of money in compensation.

But his problem was with the cut that the solicitor had taken in fees. He was alleging fraud against this particular officer of the court. He'd spoken to the Gardaí in Cork about it and they had referred him to the Fraud Squad in Dublin. After discussing the ins and outs of the case with him, I explained that he was barking up the wrong tree here. It wasn't a matter for the Fraud Squad at all. He could take it up with the Law Society if he wanted, but it definitely did not come under our remit. But there was no talking to him; he wanted to make a formal complaint. At this point, I dropped the hammer on him. 'Do you know who I am?' No, he didn't. I said I'm Superintendent Willie McGee and I met you in Macroom garda station about four years ago. Do you remember that? There was silence at the other end, so I prompted him a bit further. You were in claiming that the guards had stolen ten thousand pounds of your money. Do you remember now? There was another long, stunned silence on the line. And without saying another word, he hung up.

But I hadn't heard the last from this peculiar padre and he hadn't heard the last from me. I joined AXA Insurance in 2002 and a few years later I was down in Cork giving a fraud awareness presentation to staff in our branch office there. We had a Q&A afterwards and one of the staff members asked if she could discuss a specific case. She was finding it a bit awkward and a bit embarrassing because there was a priest making a claim and despite her telling him that he had no basis to make a claim whatsoever, he was insisting on going ahead with it. He'd actually said to her that if AXA contested it, they'd lose it because he was a priest and who would doubt his word? Said I to her, 'Is his name Fr Davern by any chance?' She got an awful surprise. It was the very same man. I told her there was only one priest I knew who would even attempt to pull a stunt like that. I gave her the background and then I told her to put in a call to him and casually mention my name. It might ring a bell with him. So she phoned him in my presence and put him on loudspeaker and told him she'd taken advice on the matter from AXA's head of fraud, Willie McGee. You might know him, Father, he used to be head of the Garda Fraud Squad. Once again, there was another pause on the line. Then he started stuttering and stumbling and saying he was never going to make a claim, he was only making inquiries about a claim. And the conversation ended fairly abruptly after that.

May God forgive me, but I must say I took great pleasure in softening his cough, not once but twice in the years after our first skirmish in Macroom. He was an unbelievably arrogant man. And it stuck with me, the day when I had to tell him that the DPP wasn't going ahead with the prosecution against him. He couldn't conceal his smugness when I told him, like he'd got one up on me and he was rubbing it in. And now it must have seemed to him that every time he was trying one of his scams, I was turning up like a bad penny to haunt him. As the man said, it's a long road that has no turning.

The more I found out about Davern, the more it became clear what a strange and unpleasant man he was. It seemed wherever he went there was aggravation and litigation with many people, up to and including his bosses in the Dioceses of Cork and Ross. From 1998 on they refused to give him an appointment in any parish and in 2003 Bishop John Buckley issued a decree prohibiting him from exercising his ministry, which meant he could no longer conduct Mass or the other sacraments. Bishop Buckley subsequently said that 'a long list of highly publicised incidents of conflict between Fr Davern and parishioners arose in successive parishes. These included a court conviction in 1999 for threatening use of a fire-arm against a member of the faithful.'

Davern had appeared in Clonakilty District Court in 1999 on charges relating to a series of incidents in Kilbrittain two years earlier. He was convicted on a charge of producing a single-barrelled shotgun in a manner likely to intimidate, and on a charge of threatening and abusive behaviour. There was also a long legal battle over the will of a local widow. She had instructed that half of her estate should go to her parish of Ballinspittle and the other half to Davern. According to various accounts, Davern took a liberal interpretation of this bequest. Cattle belonging to the lady were sold by him with no accountability for the proceeds and there was further dispute when he sought to have the licence for a shotgun belonging to her deceased husband transferred into his name. The litigation over the will dragged on for more than a decade. Eventually Davern was arrested over it. This was in 2008 and he was in hospital at the time. He was brought to Cork Circuit Civil Court where relatives of the woman said they did not wish to see him sent to jail. They just wanted land certificates that he had refused to hand over for years. But it took the threat of jail for him to finally hand them over. He ended up having to pay all the costs of this marathon legal battle.

Alongside that was a parallel legal campaign against his diocesan superiors that culminated in a ruling from the Vatican itself. He worked his way through nine different firms of solicitors and had also taken the case to the Services Industrial Professional and Technical Union (SIPTU), the Amalgamated Transport and General Workers' Union (ATGWU), the Equality Tribunal and the Department of Social Welfare. He had pursued the diocese for loss of earnings after being denied a clerical appointment in 1998. The bishop had ordered Davern to leave his parish house in Cork city and move to accommodation reserved for priests out of ministry. Davern refused, his income was severed, and thus began another legal saga. In 2006 a decree came down from the Congregation for the Clergy in Rome that the decision to remove him from ministry was 'null and void'. So Davern actually took it all the way to the Vatican and won, albeit that the diocese said it would not restore his salary nor pay him the arrears he was claiming since 1998.

He also went to the Gardaí and made a statement alleging he'd been physically assaulted while a teenage schoolboy at Farranferris College in the 1960s. He made a further allegation concerning sexual assault too. The complaints were investigated by the guards and the Diocese of Cork and Ross, but they couldn't substantiate them. He brought the complaints to the Laffoy Commission, which had been established by the government in 1999 to investigate cases of historical child abuse in a range of Irish institutions. The Commission did not find any evidence to support the complaints.

Long before all this, Davern had been ministering in Ballinspittle parish when a few local people thought they saw the statue to Our Lady moving there, in 1985. This apparent miracle soon became an international phenomenon. Hundreds of thousands of people from home and abroad flocked to witness it for themselves over the coming months and years. The Bible says you cannot serve God and mammon, but Davern made a fair effort at serving both, with mammon winning on points a lot of the time. Years later, after I had my dealings with him, I often wondered if he had somehow been behind this craze that had descended on the village – it was great for business, after all. But no, apparently not. He poured cold water on the whole thing when he was asked about it by a visiting American journalist in 1985. 'I couldn't perceive anything supernatural there,' he said. 'I failed to see any movement, even with high-powered binoculars. The statue does not move. If the grotto committee would put a bright spotlight on it – as I have asked – the alleged movements would cease.' He seemingly found the mammon aspect to it distasteful. 'Their stewards stop traffic at strategic points so the shopkeepers can benefit. It's sickening how they have commercialised it so quickly.' Pardon my cynicism, but I couldn't help thinking he was more jealous than offended.

Fr James Davern died in 2017 and doubtless went straight to heaven.

12

FORE!

The distribution manager of a sports equipment company in Portlaoise took a call one day from a man looking to buy ten sets of Spalding Top Flite golf clubs. This was the late 1980s. The Spalding was a popular, big-selling brand in the golf market back then and ten new sets was a substantial order.

The fella on the line introduced himself as Michael Wilson. He said he was a businessman and he needed the equipment for a promotion he was organising for potential customers in the Green Isle Hotel, that well-known landmark on the Naas Road coming out of Dublin. The price was discussed, a bit of haggling was done and an agreement was reached. The Portlaoise office had to call back with a few queries regarding the order, but the land-line number they rang was constantly engaged. When they checked with Telecom Éireann they were informed that the number in question was no longer in operation. Wilson subsequently called them back and apologised, explaining that he'd forgotten to mention that the phone line was having technical difficulties. He then floated the proposal that he might pay for the goods in cash, on the spot in the Green Isle, if this would be acceptable to the vendor? No problem at all, said the distribution manager in Portlaoise. He would bring the equipment personally himself to the hotel and they would complete the transaction later that evening.

Wilson sounded delighted with this arrangement. What he didn't know was that the distribution manager was a retired detective sergeant by the name of Phil O'Keeffe. And Phil hadn't come down in the last shower. He sensed from the first minute of the first phone call that this fella was dodgy; there was some sort of scam being attempted here. The next phone call he made was to the Fraud Squad where I was now a detective sergeant. Phil and myself thrashed it out on the phone; I suggested we set up a sting and he was up for it too. He would meet Mr Wilson as planned. I would scramble a crew of detectives; we had about four hours to put the operation in place. At this stage we didn't know who this conman was, we just knew his real name wasn't Michael Wilson. Other than that, I figured that either he or a few of his accomplices would be familiar to us from the ranks of the criminal class. And one or two of us would be familiar to them too.

Detective John McCann would meet up with Phil in Newbridge and join him in the van for the rest of the journey. Phil needed back-up and John would pose as his helper; we were pretty sure the criminals wouldn't recognise him. The rest of us would take up our positions a good hour before the appointed time. There was a large, mature tree directly opposite the Green Isle. Detective Joe McCarthy volunteered to climb it and hide in the foliage for a good overview of the premises. Myself and Willie Maher parked up about a half mile from the hotel, on the Naas side. We put two more men in a machinery yard about one hundred yards from the hotel. They were parked at the back of the yard and well away from the road. We had another detective floating around the vicinity on a bicycle. And finally, we had Mick Bolton dressed up as a priest – 'Father Mick' – who would take a seat in the foyer with a pot of tea and a newspaper. We were all set up in good time for the rendezvous, everyone connected by walkie talkies.

And we weren't long there before Joe Mac spotted someone driving a car from his vantage point high up in the tree. It was none other than Seán 'Fixer' Fitzgerald, a particularly unpleasant chap who'd been skulking around the underworld for years but had proven to be very elusive when it came to pinning anything on him. He had arrived early too, in order to suss out the scene and check for any signs of police surveillance. Sitting in the passenger seat was a fella we didn't recognise but would soon find out was known as Froggy Kelly. They pulled in close to the hotel and kept it under observation for about fifteen minutes; they had sight of people coming in and out through the front doors plus the traffic exiting and entering the car park. My car was too far away to be spotted by them. At one stage they drove into the machinery yard and if they kept going, they'd have spotted our lads at the far end, but they turned around and came back out again. They circled the block surrounding the hotel three times before pulling in again outside the hotel.

A few minutes later, the van from Portlaoise pulled into the car park. Phil and John McCann were no sooner in the front door than they were met by a fella who introduced himself and explained he was there in lieu of Michael Wilson. Michael had been called away on urgent business and he was there to deputise for him. We subsequently established that this fella was Jim Dunne; he was basically a go-fer, a runner for Fitzgerald. Phil and McCann played along. Dunne explained that there'd been another hitch too: they weren't able to come up with the cash, so would a bank draft do instead? Phil hummed and hawed before agreeing. Dunne was nervous, stumbling over his words, so the look of delight on his face when Phil agreed to take the draft was priceless. All that was left to do now was to hand over the merchandise. Phil and John carted in the Spalding bags with their shining sets of golf clubs into the foyer and left them with their new custodian. Dunne shook hands with them and the duo departed. They got back into the delivery van and exited the car park. Fitzgerald pulled out behind them a few seconds later. He was tailing them. We could see this happening and we alerted McCann in the passenger seat. The van kept going out the Naas Road. Fitzgerald and Kelly shadowed them as far as the Newbridge exit, obviously calculating at this point that all was well – the businessman and his helper were heading back to Portlaoise.

Meanwhile, back in the Green Isle, Dunne was clearly biding his time too, waiting until a suitable period had elapsed before putting the next phase into operation. Presumably he was waiting for Fitzgerald and Kelly to circle back to the hotel. At this stage our man in the foyer in the white collar, 'Father Mick', had inveigled his way into conversation with Dunne. This was a ploy we used with good success over the years, getting a detective dressed up as a priest to get close to criminals we were trailing.

Another colleague, Pat, acted the part brilliantly one time in Wynn's Hotel on Abbey Street. Pat was a great character and a very funny man. On this particular day, he positioned himself very discreetly into an armchair, ordered his pot of tea and took out his priest's breviary to read. From there he eavesdropped on two well-known criminals in neighbouring chairs who were discussing the logistics of an upcoming robbery, oblivious to the angelic padre beside them. He duly alerted the serious crime squad who successfully arrested the criminals on the job in question. On that occasion, as 'Father Mick' exited our office in Harcourt Square he met the chief on the steps, who addressed him with a 'Hello, Father', not realising he was a member dressed up and much to the amusement of Pat.

There was something about the priest's collar that encouraged people to drop their guard and Jim Dunne in the Green Isle Hotel that day was no different. He was giddy with excitement at how well the scam had gone and happy to talk away to 'Father Mick' about the golf clubs and how nice they were and how he was looking after them until his boss came to collect them for a promotion he was organising.

Fitzgerald and Kelly arrived back in the car park of the Green Isle. This was Dunne's cue to go over to reception and order a taxi. About five minutes later a big taxi van arrived; the driver came into the foyer and he and Dunne started lugging the golf bags out to the vehicle. And this was our cue to move. I radioed the two lads in the machinery yard to get cracking; they landed round to the front of the hotel in seconds and blocked the taxi. Myself and Willie Maher sprang for the car park, but when Fitzgerald saw us coming, he hit the accelerator and roared off in the other direction. There was a back exit to the car park and in a flash, he was gone through it. I panicked for a moment. I was effing and blinding; I thought he was gone. But lo and behold, he took a wrong turn out of the car park and ended up in a building site with no way out. He abandoned the car and started running and it was only then we noticed he had his dog with him, who was running and barking alongside him. Froggy, we discovered, wasn't a runner; he decided to hide under another car on the building site. At this stage our detective on his bicycle, Pat Collins, had got to the scene ahead of us and he was able to tell us where Kelly was hiding under the car. He continued the chase of Fitzgerald while we stopped to arrest Kelly. By now 'Father Mick' and Joe Mac, who'd been up the tree, were also in pursuit of Fitzgerald. He kept running until he could run no more. He hid behind a three-foot wall not far from Clondalkin village. Pat Collins had stayed on the trail and when his two colleagues arrived, they closed in on their quarry. Joe Mac approached the wall and there was Fitzgerald cowering on the other side holding onto his dog. Joe, like a few of us, had previous encounters with Fitzgerald and knew how to deal with him.

So, says Joe to him, 'What are you doing here, Seán?' Often when you catch a criminal red-handed, they'll come out with the first thing they can think of, no matter how ludicrous it is. Anything but admit the truth, even if it's staring everyone in the face. The best that Fitzgerald could muster was that he was out walking his dog and his dog wanted to take a dump and he needed to take a dump too and that's why they ended up behind the wall. Thankfully there was no sign that either man or beast had made a deposit al fresco, as it were. But Fitzgerald had been caught with his trousers down metaphorically speaking and there was no chance of him bluffing his way out of this corner. Joe pointed out to him that he was doing an awful lot of running and sweating for a fella who was out walking his dog; and why were his shoes and pants covered in muck? Fitzgerald quick enough of him retorted to Joe that if he had a dog who liked to run around mucky fields, his pants and shoes would be dirty too. Joe asked him if he thought the judge would believe his story and then arrested him. Man and dog were conveyed to Clondalkin garda station. Back at the Green Isle, Jim Dunne was arrested. The taxi driver, after questioning, was let go. Phil O'Keeffe and John McCann had doubled back from the Naas Road. The golf clubs were kept as evidence.

Back in headquarters we prepared the files on the three defendants. They were charged with the same crimes: false pretences and forgery. Young Jim Dunne decided to plead guilty in the District Court and got the Probation Act having no previous convictions. We were happy enough with that; we knew he was just a pawn in the grander scheme. Froggy Kelly was in trouble from the moment it emerged that his phone calls to the Portlaoise office had been recorded. He had posed as 'Michael Wilson' but, unfortunately for him, he possessed a particularly high-pitched tone of voice. It was distinctive, kind of screechy, and a few detectives who'd come across him previously knew that the voice on the phone recordings could only belong to Froggy. They would testify as such in court if needed. Obviously, there was all the other evidence garnered from the day of the operation too, but the sound of his squeaky voice on the phone calls seemingly persuaded him to plead guilty and take his punishment. He got a light sentence as he hadn't been a very active criminal and wasn't the main conspirator in this case either.

Fitzgerald on the other hand decided to try and brazen it out. He opted for a trial by jury in the Circuit Court. He was hoping to catch a break somewhere along the way, a loophole or flaw in the prosecution evidence unearthed by his lawyers, or a witness becoming unavailable, or some other happenstance of the judicial system. He had form in getting away on previous charges over the years and figured he might repeat the trick again. And one reason he'd escaped jail before was because he was a tout, an informant. And like a lot of touts, he wasn't a very reliable one. He'd tell you any old shite if he thought it would help him, all sorts of rumours and gossip about this criminal and that criminal, or pure fiction invented by him on the spot.

Back in his early days, we're talking the 1970s here, he used to install televisions. This was at a time when colour televisions were taking over from the old black-and-white sets. A favourite stunt of his was to rob the televisions out of the houses in which he'd previously installed them. An innocent family would spend their money on a brand-new colour TV; it would be their pride and joy, and quite an investment for people on ordinary wages back then. They would pay the installer his fee as well and if the installer was Fitzgerald, there was a good chance he'd be back a few nights later in the dead of night to rob it. Then he'd sell it on to another household at a reduced price plus the fee of installing it here too. The purchasers wouldn't necessarily know it was stolen goods. As a TV technician he could easily spin the yarn that he regularly came across second-hand TVs in good condition and people wouldn't think to query it any more than that. They were getting a bargain and they weren't going to turn it down.

But soon enough the pattern became obvious once local guards started investigating the spate of stolen televisions around Clondalkin. A lot of the houses broken into had their tellys installed by Fitzgerald in the first place. The trail led back to him. But unfortunately, a few guards decided to use him for their own gains. There was a detective sergeant who exploited information that Fitzgerald gave him to build up his own CV of successful prosecutions. Basically, it was a case of you scratch my back and I'll scratch yours. Fitzgerald gave him a number of names and addresses where he'd installed his stolen televisions. Then the detective sergeant and a few of his mates would turn up at these houses with a warrant and arrest the people for receiving stolen goods. They'd recover the televisions, return them to their rightful owners and prosecute decent people who'd bought their sets off Fitzgerald not knowing they were stolen. It was a lousy thing to do, but they did it. He had this detective sergeant wrapped round his little finger. And he had a few other guards conned as well with this kind of dirty information. They were willing to be conned for their own purposes. But that was how 'Fixer' Fitzgerald operated. He thought he was too smart for the police and in some cases he was. In fact, he was arrogant enough to ring me up a couple of times in the Fraud Squad looking to butter me up with inside information too. I told him where to go in no uncertain terms.

With his trial looming, Fitzgerald tried to wriggle his way out of it, looking for some kind of plea bargain and touting all kinds of information on other criminals. He thought his previous collaborations with various Gardaí would help him game the system again. I wasn't having any of it. His legal team put us all through the wringer in the witness box and generally tried to sow as much confusion as possible with the jury. But the good and true people of the jury didn't buy it. The day they came back in with a unanimous guilty verdict on all counts, he nearly died of shock. I could see it in his face. He was stunned. At that point I had the opportunity, at long last, to tell the judge who this guy really was and I took great pleasure in so doing. This fella had evaded justice for so long it was ridiculous, but he'd finally gotten his comeuppance. The judge sentenced him to three years in jail and he was led away shellshocked, white in the face. We all repaired to the Legal Eagle afterwards to celebrate a job well done. A lot of us took great pleasure in seeing him sent down.

Fitzgerald gave me a filthy look as he was led away in handcuffs that day. He took it personally against me I suppose because I was absolutely immune to his lies and games. We crossed paths several times in the next decade and more. He was actually a friendly, civil kind of fella in these interactions. There was never a threat of violence or anything of that nature. He was usually dressed in suits and presented himself as a polite, clean-cut businessman. And occasionally he'd tell me in the friendliest way possible that he hated my guts but admired my stubbornness in pursuing him, and other criminals that he knew, without fear or favour.

He actually tried to pull one of his touting stunts when he was serving time for the golf clubs con job. A detective colleague of mine approached me one day to say he'd been summoned to Mountjoy Prison by Fitzgerald on the promise of information about the infamous Beit robbery. This was the robbery in 1986 of several priceless paintings from the collection owned by Sir Alfred Beit at his home, Russborough House near Blessington in Co. Wicklow. It was the largest art robbery in the history of the State. Martin Cahill, the so-called General, was the criminal head honcho who'd pulled it off. At the time it made headlines around the world and the Irish police were under pressure for years after to try and solve it and retrieve the paintings. So, of course, Fitzgerald knew this and tried to dangle a juicy carrot in front of us: information that could lead to the recovery of the paintings. It would be a major coup for any policeman who could crack the case. Naturally the quid pro quo for Fitzgerald would be an early release from prison. I discussed his offer with my chief superintendent in the Fraud Squad and we decided to sup with a long spoon when it came to this particular negotiation. Fitzgerald wanted to part with his information after we established an early release date for him. His excuse was that he couldn't trust us; if he traded the information first, we could throw away the key; we could leave him to rot in his cell while taking credit for this massive breakthrough in the Beit investigation. In reality, it was us who couldn't trust him; we couldn't trust him as far as we could throw him. We needed to see the colour of his money first and we relayed that condition back to him loud and clear: tell us what you know and if it's any good, we'll see if we can get you out early. Inevitably, he couldn't back up his promises. He knew sweet feck all about the robbery or where the paintings were. And we knew that if we agreed to his conditions, he'd play a long game with us on the outside that would lead to nothing but a bottle of smoke. Basically, he was bullshitting us and if we'd let him out early, he'd have been boasting and bragging all over town about how he'd hoodwinked the cops again. Fitzgerald did his time in the Joy before resuming his life of crime.

In the meantime, I was promoted to Garda Inspector and transferred out of the Fraud Squad to the L District, which covered Ballyfermot, Ronanstown, Clondalkin and Lucan stations. There was always trouble going on in

Ronanstown in particular. You had stolen cars and all sorts of crimes of every description to deal with virtually every single day. Car chases were a common occurrence. There was one little runt of about fifteen or sixteen and he could barely see out over the top of the steering wheel, but he was an absolute menace; he had no sense of right or wrong and no sense of danger either to himself or others. He was addicted to stealing cars and driving them at crazy speeds around the streets. It didn't matter who was in the way. On three or four separate occasions he rammed straight into Garda cars and managed to get out and run away.

I remember one time there was a patrol car pulled in on the side of the street; the driver and his partner in the passenger seat were talking to two fellas who'd been up before the courts on many occasions. And next thing this big Ford came tearing down the street and heading straight for the patrol car. The two fellas saw it coming and managed to jump out of the way, but the two guards were sitting ducks. Your man kept going and rammed full speed into the patrol car. The two guards were badly injured; they could have been killed stone dead. The squad car was written off. This gouger was arrested and brought in for questioning several times, but he didn't care one iota. He'd sit in the interview room laughing at us; it was a total waste of time trying to talk a bit of sense into him. We regularly searched the house he lived in and that didn't bother him one whit either. He was feral, wild; there was just no getting through to him.

And the thing was, when it came to him stealing cars, it was hard to pin him down on anything because, literally, you couldn't see him behind the steering wheel. I remember one of the lads who'd been in a car chase with him saying you'd think there was nobody driving the car because he was so small. With the head rest behind him and the steering wheel in front of him, you couldn't make him out. He was a skinny, insignificant little gurrier who got his kicks out of speed and danger. It was the likes of him that made life a misery for so many decent people living in those communities. I met some of the nicest people you'd ever come across anywhere in Ronanstown and Clondalkin. The anti-social behaviour they had to put up with often caused them terrible stress; they were constantly worried for their children and their own security. I remember one case of a man, I think he was a prison officer in Wheatfield, who spotted a bunch of youths loitering around his car one day. He came out and they were totally brazen with him and he chased them away with a few threats. An hour later his car was on fire. When we called round, he was badly shaken. One of the arsonists was the same little toerag we'd been dealing with for months on end.

For a finish, he didn't last long enough to inflict much more destruction. He met his end the way it was always going to end, with one kamikaze mission too many. It happened during another night-time and another car chase. This time he took off in a stolen car down the Naas Road with two or three passengers for company and a couple of patrol cars after him. He lost control of the vehicle and crashed into the back of a truck at a massive speed, maybe 150mph. The guards pulled everyone from the wreckage; miraculously they were all alive and more or less unscathed. They arrested the young fellas, then the car was put up onto a tow truck and impounded. It was the dark of night. Next morning when they went to do an inspection of the wrecked motor, they found the driver dead in the footwell under the steering wheel. The arrested boys had never mentioned him to the guards. Basically, what happened was the car ploughed into the back of the truck and had its roof nearly sheared off. The driver must have slid under the steering wheel to try and protect himself but was crushed completely by the impact. He was so small that he'd been able to fold himself into the footwell and no one noticed him that night in the dark. They found him in the morning dead as doornails. In all honesty, no one in the garda stations shed a tear for him; we were glad to see the back of him. He had nearly killed a couple of our colleagues; he had come close to mowing down innocent pedestrians on a number of occasions. He was a scourge and a scumbag and nobody I knew was sorry to see him gone.

While I was in L District as a uniformed inspector, a vacancy came up for detective inspector; I applied and was appointed. I was only about three months in my new post when Pat Byrne rang me one day and asked if I would take over a new anti-racketeering unit (ARU). Pat was well advanced in the Garda hierarchy at the time and would go on to become Garda Commissioner. We had no ARU back then but under EU regulations we were required to set one up. Racketeering was just another form of organised crime and one of my first investigations was a big video piracy operation. These criminals were flooding the market with cheap copies of the popular films of the day. The ARU found the headquarters in a residential house where there were thousands of bootleg videos and a number of machines copying them onto blank tapes.

I was only about six months in the ARU when Fachtna Murphy contacted me and asked if I'd go back to the Garda Bureau of Fraud Investigation as detective inspector. Fachtna in due course would go on to become Garda Commissioner too. I was happy to return to my old stomping ground and would spend the next year of my service as a detective inspector there until I was promoted to superintendent and transferred to Macroom, Co. Cork. After a year in Cork, I returned once more to take up the position of detective superintendent or Deputy Director of the Garda Bureau of Fraud Investigations.

13

OPERATION BRIDGE

During the 1990s a remarkable run of unfortunate road traffic accidents occurred in Longford and its environs.

Many of them were two-car collisions, some were single car, occasionally they were three-car events. A lot of cars were being stolen too. Some of the incidents happened in Dublin. A large majority of the damaged vehicles ended up in a motor centre in Longford town, next door to Pearse Park, the GAA grounds on the Sligo Road. The business was owned by one Michael Byrne of Newtownforbes, Co. Longford. Byrne ran a number of companies from his premises there, including Lough Forbes Filling Station, a Peugeot dealership, a Rover dealership and Longford Crash Repairs.

Michael Byrne's businesses had been central to many claims which were described in court at his sentencing as scams which amounted to a sustained and organised conspiracy against a number of insurers, in particular the company then widely known as PMPA, now AXA Insurance. Mostly it involved the staging of car accidents, using previously crashed cars and claiming money for newer models of the exact same cars. The charges also included falsely reporting that a car had been stolen and using the names of innocent parties without their knowledge in making some of these claims. He was prosecuted for offences between 1994 and 1996; these had cost PMPA almost £324,000. But in reality, the company had traced over eighty suspect claims going back to 1990; they paid out almost £1.3 million in the space of that six years.

By the mid-nineties the Garda Fraud Squad had been called in. It began with a local guard in Longford smelling a rat. He was called to the scene of an accident one day. The driver showed him the damage to the car. But unfortunately for this particular chap, the guard in question had trained as a mechanic before joining the force. He knew what he was looking at. And he knew he wasn't looking at a freshly damaged car. He was looking at old damage that the motorist was passing off as new. The Garda reported back to his station and it triggered suspicions among other Gardaí about previous accidents that they'd attended. They started combing the Garda computer system for Longford and surrounding areas. A pattern started to emerge: many of the accidents happened in more or less the same way. And virtually every car involved had been taken to Michael Byrne's crash repairs facility. So they started re-examining previous cases and the more they looked, the more it snowballed.

The area commanding officer and the chief super-intendent in Mullingar garda station, were informed. When they read the reports, it was decided to call in the Garda Bureau of Fraud Investigation and after an initial conference on the matter it was decided that a major investigation would have to be mounted with substantial resources in terms of time, manpower and budget. We requested and got representatives from Sligo, Leitrim and Louth as well as Longford, such was the scale of the crime going on. The operation was codenamed 'Operation Bridge' and the Fraud Squad would head up the investigation. I detailed two of my leading detective inspectors, two detective sergeants and six detective Gardaí to take command of the operation.

An operational hub was required – a dedicated office for the task – and it was decided that we would set up in Carrick-on-Shannon garda station. The Board of Works was commissioned to prepare a room in the station. Security was a concern. A couple of criminals involved in the scam were Irish Republican Army (IRA) patriots. The entrance doors to the office would be fortified with steel; the glass in the windows would be reinforced; fireproofed safes would be needed for holding the evidence in case anyone decided to burn the building.

It took ten years to see it through – the last court case was heard in 2006. The time period would straddle my last remaining years in the Garda Bureau and my first years heading up a new fraud investigations unit in AXA Insurance – the company formerly known as PMPA. During that decade, almost 1,300 statements were taken; thirty-five people were arrested and nineteen prosecuted. It was a conspiracy of fraud on a grand scale; it included a member of the Garda Síochána, a number of PMPA's own assessors, an auctioneer, a plant hire contractor, a golfer, a housewife, an accountant, farmers, businessmen, company directors and car salesmen. They were described by a judge as 'willing volunteers who were not forced into the fraud which was masterminded by an individual and was calculated, deliberate and sophisticated'.

Some ten years before it was subsumed into AXA Insurance, PMPA was taken over by the British insurer Guardian Royal Exchange, around 1989/90. When we alerted PMPA in Dublin about the scale of the conspiracy we were uncovering, they passed it on to Guardian Royal's company HQ in England. What really worried them was the suspicion that a number of their own assessors on the ground, who were there to protect the company from fraudulent claims, had gone over to the other side. These employees were colluding in the scams and creaming off their cut of the proceeds. Management in England became so alarmed at what they were hearing, they decided to send over their own special investigations unit. They landed in late '96 and liaised with us and began building their own picture. They compiled a detailed report for their bosses back at headquarters in the spring of '97.

'There are numerous claims', said the report, 'involving insured persons and third parties who are identified as members of the extended Byrne family, associates, employees and friends. Examination of the files reveals that they make claims against their own policies, and appear as third party claimants against other policies.' The report also noted some of the explanations offered by the various drivers in their claim forms. 'The circumstances given for the causes of accidents are many and varied, including three swerving to avoid badgers, avoiding a fox and other animals, a dog barking in the car, and switching on the radio to listen to the Eurovision Song Contest.'

One of the first family members to be prosecuted was a married mother of two children who was eventually jailed for three years in 2004 for staging an accident in 1994 and fraudulently claiming €8,840 from Guardian PMPA as a result.

A member of An Garda Síochána was also caught up in those scams. He was stationed in Carrick-on-Shannon at that time and had the uncanny knack of being on duty on the days when a number of accidents occurred. He was thus able to arrive swiftly on the scene and was available to record the necessary details before filing an official report. The same reports would then be used to verify the details and authenticate claims when required by insurance companies. This particular Garda would use the reports to exaggerate and falsify details where necessary to ensure a payout from the insurance company. He was jailed for three years and in sentencing him the judge commented that it was 'a disgraceful act' and that 'the greatest indignity for a member of An Garda Síochána is to serve time behind bars'.

A Leitrim farmer and his brother – a company director in Longford – were both sentenced for their part in several accidents involving heavy machinery and a low loader. The farmer received a two-year sentence, but his brother, the businessman, decided to fight the cases, alleging the delays experienced in waiting for trial caused the aggravation of his blood pressure and brought on liver and ulcer problems. The State's counter-argument was that much of the delay was unavoidable due to the complexity of the overall situation. Operation Bridge was dealing with eighty interconnected cases involving over 1,000 civilian witnesses and over 100 bank accounts. It was just a mammoth task trying to process them all and get them to court.

The businessman's trial went ahead before a jury at the Dublin Circuit Criminal Court. In evidence it was revealed that for one of the accidents a car had been placed on the wrong side of the road and around a bend by an accomplice, who had already confessed to his role in the scam. One of the detectives from the Fraud Squad told the court that Guardian/PMPA had paid out over £70,000 as a result of the accident. Of this, the defendant received a cheque for £56,000 which he deposited in a bank account linked to Michael Byrne. 'That's not to say he [the defendant] didn't receive anything,' added the detective. The court also heard that when the man was first questioned by Gardaí, he remarked: 'It looks bad for me doesn't it?'

The jury found him guilty as charged. As part of his plea for leniency, an entourage of supporters lined up as character witnesses on his behalf. These included his parish priest, his doctor, the mayor of Longford county council, a senior official in Longford county council, the retired deputy principal of the local community school, a retired Garda and the area manager of a local bank.

The judge imposed a two-year jail sentence. He said that despite the testimonials on the defendant's behalf, he could not ignore that it had been a carefully planned conspiracy, not something done on impulse.

Time does not diminish the gravity of this matter or the calculated manner in which it was conceived and executed. I have a duty to let it be known from this court that a crime where there is planning and calculation is a grave matter because it can have an effect on the community by increasing [insurance] premiums whereas otherwise they would remain at a lower level.

Also caught up in the trawl was an auctioneer from Westmeath. He was involved in a number of claims from a variety of situations: a rear-ended car, a stolen car and a car going on fire. Like many of the other cases in Operation Bridge, this one dragged on for years. The defendant went to the High Court to have proceedings against him aborted on the grounds of excessive delay in prosecuting the case. Again, the judge refused this application. It was only when he knew the jig was up that the auctioneer pleaded guilty, to three charges of fraud and false pretences, rather than go through the embarrassing publicity that would come with a full trial. He also brought €7,000 to the court in offer as compensation. The judge was unmoved by the gesture, saying the defendant had lied to Gardaí repeatedly and his guilty plea had only come at the eleventh hour. 'The court is not impressed by the last-minute attempts to offer compensation in this case and as I'm imposing a custodial sentence, I will not accept the €7,000 offered here today.' The auctioneer was convicted in the Dublin Circuit Criminal Court of a number of crimes and was sentenced to thirty months in prison.

What finally tripped up Michael Byrne was a staged accident involving three cars on a slip road to the M50 at Lucan in December 1994. One of the parties in this event was a golfer who Byrne had hired in 1992 to run a driving range he'd opened in Longford. As part of his contract, the golfer was able to drive cars from Byrne's Rover and Peugeot dealerships. On the day in question, the golfer was in Dublin driving a Peugeot 605. Michael Byrne told him to pull into the car park of the Foxhunter pub in Lucan and wait there. Another man came along and told the golfer to get into the passenger seat. This man then drove the Peugeot onto the slip road and pulled up right behind a parked Rover 218, touching the rear bumper. Then a Mercedes 300 came along and rear-ended the Peugeot which in turn rear-ended the Rover. Gardaí came along, the details were taken and a report was drafted. Claims from a number of connected parties were submitted to PMPA and a total of £30,659.85 was paid into bank accounts controlled by Byrne.

The golfer pleaded guilty to his part in the fraud in the District Court and was given the Probation Act. His evidence helped to build the case against Michael Byrne, who eventually faced justice at the Dublin Circuit Criminal Court in October 2002. One of the charges against Byrne concerned a Citroen that the golfer was driving on 28 May 1995, which broke down near Athlone. The golfer contacted Byrne, who told him that he should report the car as stolen. Byrne instructed him to turn up at the Red Cow Inn on 14 June, then contact the Gardaí from there and tell them the car had been stolen. The golfer did as he was told and officers from Clondalkin garda station came to the scene and logged the details. The Citroen turned up days later with some damage done to it. It was insured by the Irish National Insurance Company. The golfer filled out a claim form and monies were paid to a solicitor. Byrne was charged with attempting to obtain money from the Irish National Insurance Company by falsely claiming a car was stolen.

As for the three-car collision on the M50 slip road, Byrne was found guilty of conspiring together with others to defraud PMPA. The jury was divided on the charge against Byrne relating to the stolen Citroen. The case was adjourned for sentencing to the following month. Byrne had pleaded not guilty to the charges but, having already been found guilty of the M50 incident, he decided to plead guilty to additional charges which were looming against him, relating to falsely obtaining money from the PMPA and Cornhill Insurance for a further series of accidents staged at various locations between 1994 and 1996. On 22 November 2002, Judge Yvonne Murphy sentenced him to two six-year terms, with three years suspended in each case. She further sentenced him to three terms of four years, with the final two years suspended in each case. All the sentences were to run concurrently.

Byrne had lodged €50,000 with the court. Judge Murphy commended the Gardaí for their 'exemplary work' in the case and directed that €5,000 of the €50,000 should go to the Garda Benevolent Fund, with the balance going to PMPA. I was in court that day and conveyed the €50,000 back to AXA Insurance and ensured that the €5,000 was forwarded to the benevolent fund.

There was a further blow for Michael Byrne when the Director for Public Prosecutions decided to appeal against the jail sentence handed down to him in November, on the grounds that it was 'unduly lenient'. While Byrne had been given a raft of prison terms, the net effect was that he would serve less than three years in prison. In October 2003 the three-man Court of Criminal Appeal gave its decision on the DPP's appeal. Mr Justice Murray said the court was taking into account a number of mitigating factors put forward on Byrne's behalf, not least the fact that he had, in effect, 'lost everything'. He had lost his business and his standing in the community. On the other hand, the frauds perpetrated were 'calculated, deliberate and sophisticated'. They involved careful preparation of a plan that created the circumstances where it would be believed that a road traffic accident had taken place, and that serious damage had been caused to particular vehicles and in some cases to individuals.

Justice Murray's description of the scams as 'calculated, deliberate and sophisticated' chimed with the findings of the special investigations unit sent over from England by Guardian Royal Exchange. In their 1997 report they point out that several of the more costly bogus claims have

> received careful scrutiny before payments have
> been made, including interviews of the insured
> persons and witnesses by Claims Inspectors,
> but there has been no good reason to refuse the

claim. Gardaí enquiries lead them to believe that a good deal of effort has been put into briefing claimants and producing supporting evidence, such as photographs of the scene supplied by the perpetrators.

In other words, it was not an amateur operation. We were all to discover that as we set about our investigations.

Anyway, Justice Murray and his two fellow judges in the Court of Criminal Appeal accepted the DPP's appeal. He said that Byrne's knowledge and experience in the motor trade had underpinned the frauds. He would have had access to crashed vehicles in order to mount the series of offences in which he engaged. The appeal court was therefore satisfied that the sentences imposed in the circuit court were unduly lenient. It ordered that Byrne's time in prison be extended from three years to five.

The cases cited here were among the biggest to be uncovered by Operation Bridge. But in reality, they were only the tip of a very large iceberg. Dozens upon dozens more, involving hundreds of other people, were uncovered but not prosecuted due to insufficient evidence or because the insurance companies decided to write them off and move on. The sheer quantity of cases meant that it just wasn't possible to pursue every suspect claim to the end of the line. A lot of otherwise law-abiding citizens had been involved in one way or another, looking for some free money from what they considered to be victimless crimes. But money is never free and those who were caught paid a severe price for thinking that it was.

14

THE TAOISIGH

The late 1990s were notable for me for one other reason too. In February 1997 the Taoiseach John Bruton appointed Mr Justice Brian McCracken as the sole member of a tribunal of inquiry to investigate some pretty high-profile accusations. It was alleged that a businessman called Mr Ben Dunne had been making payments to politicians which had gone undeclared. The tribunal was to enquire into all payments made directly or indirectly by Mr Ben Dunne to politicians or political parties between 1986 and 1996.

All members of the Dáil and Senate were contacted with a pro forma letter asking if they had received any payments from Mr Dunne. All replied in the negative, including Mr Charles J. Haughey; he denied that he or anyone connected to him had received any payment from Mr Ben Dunne.

Over the course of 1997, several letters were received by the tribunal from Haughey wherein he again denied receiving any payments. All the letters were personally signed 'Charles J. Haughey'.

When the tribunal concluded, Mr McCracken stated that Mr Haughey's attitude during the tribunal was such that it might amount to an offence or offences constituting obstruction under the Tribunal of Inquiry (Evidence) Act. It was also stated that the tribunal could not accept or believe much of Haughey's evidence. As such, the relevant papers were forwarded to the Director of Public Prosecutions (DPP), Mr Hamilton, who referred them to the Garda Commissioner. He, in turn, referred them to the Garda Bureau of Fraud Investigations and that was how both myself and Det. Supt Pat Brehony became involved in trying to establish if the former Taoiseach should be prosecuted as alleged in the tribunal report.

Numerous meetings were held with the DPP's office; their representative, senior counsel Mr Maurice Gaffney, took the lead and advised us accordingly.

Both Pat and I met Mr Haughey and his legal team at his home in Kinsealy. I can recall Charlie himself pouring out cups of coffee for us from his silver coffee pot and drinking from beautiful China mugs. We were treated with the utmost respect and courtesy by Mr Haughey and his team of four legal advisors. They advised that Mr Haughey should make a statement to us after caution. Charlie accepted and reiterated that he sent in the letters to the tribunal.

When our interview was over, Charlie signed the statement that was taken from him, witnessed by his legal advisors.

We then brought his signature on our statement to the Garda handwriting specialists who stated that it was identical to the signatures on all the letters received by the tribunal.

Having taken the advice of Mr Gaffney and the DPP, I went to the Court Clerk's Office in Chancery Street and applied to have summonses issued against Mr Haughey as directed. Having applied for them, neither myself nor Pat Brehony, as investigating officers, could serve the summonses on Mr Haughey so I asked my detective inspector, John McKeon, to do the necessary.

John duly met Mr Haughey at his home and after identifying himself to Charlie and telling him that he had summonses to serve on him, Charlie rang his solicitor to confirm that it was okay to accept the summonses. He was also, by all accounts, preoccupied with John's name, uttering the words 'McKeon, McKeon, McKeon', trying to find out where the name McKeon originated from. John found this amusing and when he told Charlie it was Leitrim, Charlie said that he was thinking along those lines. Any time I met John afterwards and asked him to do anything for me, I would address him as 'McKeon, McKeon, McKeon' which went down well in a lighthearted fashion.

Charlie duly appeared in court in Richmond Street to answer the allegations against him and elected for trial by judge and jury. The question of jury selection was a priority. Legal submissions from the defence and prosecution teams were put to Judge Kevin Haugh to establish whether Charlie would get a fair trial and there was a questionnaire put together for potential jury members; the wording of the questionnaire needed to be proportionate, so it was not apparent if potential jury members supported Fianna Fáil or not; it was also necessary for them not to have any association with the Dunne family. The questioning of prospective jurors was a new departure and considered an unwelcome one; it coincided with the dicta in other common law countries.

However, the whole question of whether trial by jury would be fair in this case was put to rest eventually due to a statement made by Mary Harney in the Dáil stating that Mr Haughey should be jailed. This was considered by Judge Haugh to carry such weight that it may not be possible for there to be a fair trial, no matter what jury was empanelled to hear his case.

The trial was aborted and as a result Charles J. Haughey never had to answer to the allegations made against him that he was in breach of two offences under the Tribunal of Inquiry Act. Charlie walked out of court a free man.

I actually met him in the departure lounge of Dublin Airport a few months later. While I was waiting in the lounge in Dublin Airport, Charlie walked in; he spotted me and came straight over and introduced me to his wife, Maureen. He then said that since we met last, he had found out that I was a Mayoman and asked me if I was aware he was born in Castlebar. I told him I was and that I was actually at the function in the Burlington the night he was honoured as Mayoman of the year. He wished me well and stated that he knew we had a job to do and that he bore no animosity towards me or indeed any member of the Gardaí.

In that same year, 1997, another matter was brought to my attention by a bank manager who contacted me with a concern because a large amount of credit had been obtained by two men in order to finance a building project. The concern was delicate because it related to the association of one Patrick Russell with the ex-Taoiseach, Albert Reynolds.

After discussing the case with the bank manager, I suggested he inform Mr Reynolds that I would be available to meet up with him and advise him that he appeared to be going down the wrong road in his association and dealings with Mr Russell.

The bank manager met with Mr Reynolds subsequently and informed him of my offer, but the offer was flatly rejected; he retorted that if he wished to receive any such advice, he would deal with the Garda Commissioner and not a superintendent in the Fraud Squad.

I abandoned my commitment in that direction, but I did report the matter further, advising the Crime and Security Branch (CSB) commissioner about Mr Reynolds' association with Russell and another assistant whose activities were not always above board. I can only presume that my report went to the minister for justice and, in due course, to the Taoiseach, Bertie Ahern.

Russell was recently the subject of an RTÉ documentary. It outlined the extraordinary fraudulent activities he engaged in throughout his career as an accountant and barrister. Having come from a staunch Fianna Fáil generation, I trust I will be forgiven for having had to deal with two former Taoisigh in my lifetime investigating fraud.

15

OPERATION KIOSK

I got a phone call one day from a very agitated senior manager in Telecom Éireann. They were being robbed blind by a bogus premium rate service and wanted a stop put to it that very same day if possible. This was May 1998. Telecom had been paying out thousands of pounds each month for the previous twelve months and now the next payment was due. They figured they were down about £100,000 at this stage. I invited them immediately to a meeting in our headquarters in Harcourt Square to find out what was going on.

The money was going to an outfit called Netstar Communications which had been set up to offer a computer shareware service – something to do with providing computer software to customers. The main man behind it, we discovered, was named John Veldman. He was a very obese chap in his early thirties who lived with his mother in Raheny. He was a qualified computer programmer and, by all accounts, a bit of a genius in this line of work. He had originally set up his premium rate service two years earlier under the name Veldman

Computer Services (VCS). He had gone through the proper channels in setting it up. He had applied and been approved by RegTel, the regulator for premium rate telephone services that became ComReg in 2010. VCS then entered into a contract with Telecom Éireann's Telemarketing Services arm to operate the hotline. In March '97 VCS changed its name to Netstar Communications and its business address from Marrowbone Lane in Dublin 8 to the first floor of the Edenmore shopping centre in Raheny. Netstar's premium call number was 1580 145632. Every call to this number would cost the caller £1.50 per minute. Netstar would get 96.50p a minute; Telecom would get 26p with the balance going to the regulator. The 1580 number was being routed through three telephone lines to Veldman's computer. So if, for example, all three lines were operating constantly for an hour, 96.50p per minute multiplied by three is £2.89 per minute, multiplied by sixty minutes is £173.40 an hour. Multiply that by forty hours a week and you're talking serious money. Soon enough, Telecom Éireann were sending him very substantial cheques. The number and duration of every call to 1580 145632 was logged on their system and sent on a stats sheet to Netstar every month. Netstar would then invoice them and Telecom would issue a cheque. Netstar received £117,829.55 in total between March 1997 and April 1998.

By then, personnel in Telecom's information systems had noticed a highly irregular pattern. They were conducting periodic analyses on their public payphones network throughout Ireland. And they noticed that a payphone on the Howth Road had been one of the highest earning in the country over the previous twelve months. What's more, the bulk of phone calls made from this phone box was going to a premium rate service, number 1580 145632. Normally, 60 per cent of business from public payphones were just local calls. So they decided to conduct a fraud analysis on this particular 1580 number for the month of March 1998.

They found that 2,382 calls had been made to this Netstar company, and that nearly all had been made from payphones scattered around different parts of Dublin. But the callers were not using the old coin phones. They were using the card phones that had been installed in increasing numbers by Telecom from about 1990 onwards. These had become a popular alternative to the coin phones. People would buy a call card ranging in capacity from 10 units to 20 to 50 to 100, and in cost from £2 to £16. Telecom's analysts found that nearly all calls to this 1580 number lasted roughly the equivalent of a 100-unit call card; that the user in the phone kiosk would ring the same number again roughly twenty seconds after they hung up the previous one; and that three calls to the number would be happening simultaneously from three different locations.

It was all very strange. And among the questions it raised was why would people be calling a computer software service from public payphones in the first place? It didn't make sense, if you needed technical support for your computer, to be making calls from a phone kiosk when you could be making them from your home phone with your computer in front of you. When a senior manager in Telecom dialled the number, she got an automatic reply that asked for a customer PIN number, but there were no instructions as to how to get a PIN number to become a customer.

And it was at this point that we in the Fraud Squad received the call. We met them and they filled us in on the background. They wanted the meeting urgently because the next payment to Netstar, worth £20,382.74, was due to be paid. But of course, we had to put an operation in place first. We had to gather evidence and build a case. If Telecom cancelled the arrangement suddenly, the scam would disappear – and so would a lot of the evidence. So we advised them to issue the cheque as if no one had noticed anything. Sometimes they posted the cheque to Netstar, but more often Veldman would come in to collect it himself in Telecom's offices just down the road from us on Harcourt Street. He duly arrived in the next day to collect it and we had people there to video and photograph him.

Detective Sergeant Paul Gillen led the investigation with Detective Garda Noel Wade centrally involved too. Within a week we had a surveillance plan in place, based on the locations and patterns showing up in Telecom's data. We had to identify the people making the calls and to do that we had to stake out the phone boxes they were using. And in order to be able to do that, we would first have to trace the calls going to the 1580 number from all these different phone boxes. There was an awful lot of technical logistics to get your head around. For example, calls made from the 01 Dublin area code to all premium rate numbers were routed through four different telephone exchanges. Telecom's technicians fixed it that all calls to 1580 145632 would be deflected to the one exchange, in Dolphin's Barn. But the calls to this number would then have to be filtered out from all the other call traffic coming through Dolphin's Barn. So a dedicated route was established to isolate these calls to Netstar; it would have four lines in case four calls to this number were being made at the same time. Finally, and crucially, whenever and wherever the number was dialled, part of the trace system ensured that we could identify the location of the payphone. We were able to track the number of the phone being used, the date and time of the call and its duration. All of this information was logged in a database. Soon we had a pattern, a map of the call boxes.

The next step was to start surveillance exercises on these boxes. We began on 18 May and resumed on 20 and 27 May and 3 June. We assigned two members of the fraud bureau to each box. They had cameras and video equipment. The calls were monitored by Telecom personnel and as each call was activated, they would alert the detectives in their car assigned to that particular phone box. We had investigators at the telephone exchange as well listening in on the calls. Soon they started to become familiar with the voices on the line. We figured there were ten regular callers clocking up the minutes to this 1580 number. These were the runners doing the business on the ground. They quickly became familiar faces to our crews who were filming and photographing them.

They all had their own territory to cover and they were circulating around from one phone box to another in that same vicinity. Where possible, any time a suspect left the kiosk, one of our people would step in and make a call to colleagues in the telephone exchange, just to say that the suspect had left the phone box, thereby reinforcing the chain of evidence. We logged calls from nearly thirty different phone boxes during those four days.

The runners had a challenge in trying to fill the empty air time. I mean, they had to stand there talking to nobody for hours on end. Once the 100-unit card expired they'd hang up and head to another kiosk and repeat the process. If there was nobody else queuing outside to use the phone, they'd simply take out the old card and replace it with a new one and go again. But they were making zombie phone calls and if there was someone else waiting outside hopping from one foot to the other, the suspect on the phone would have to pretend he or she was talking to somebody. This led to a creativity problem, as it were. It required a bit of acting. Nearly all fraud jobs require a bit of acting at some stage. But the suspects weren't actors who could recite long passages from Shakespeare or the like. They just rambled on about anything and everything, talking about all sorts of things, much to the amusement sometimes of the Gardaí and Telecom technicians who were listening in on the other end. Our priority was to identify these callers and some of them who could think of nothing better to say would start talking about themselves. That's actually how we came to identify some of them. One of the callers gave his name, his date of birth, his mother's name, her maiden name, his father's name and his father's occupation. He said he was a student in Dublin City University (DCU) and that it was his girlfriend, who was operating another kiosk, who got him into this line of activity. He named her too and outlined her biographical details.

Another chap also helped us enormously by attending the same phone box on Stephen's Green practically every day during office hours. In fact, they were nearly all operating this scam during office hours, which made our work a lot easier. This fella was a motorcycle courier, but his bike was registered not in his name but with the courier company. So to identify him, we got a guard from the traffic bureau to make an intervention. On the appointed day, he followed the courier from Stephen's Green and pulled him in on Baggot Street, *mar dhea*, to ask him for his licence and check his insurance. This fella didn't have his documents with him but politely explained that he lived on Clanbrassil Street and if the guard wished, he could follow him back to his home on Clanbrassil Street and furnish him with the relevant papers there. This wouldn't normally be the done thing and the guard had to feign a bit of reluctance before agreeing. Yer man led him home and duly supplied the details. Job done.

Time was ticking now because the next payment to Netstar Communications would be due shortly again. On 11 June, 'Operation Kiosk' swung into action. I suppose the name is self-explanatory. It was one of the most fulfilling days I ever had in the job. There was about eighty staff in the Garda Bureau of Fraud Investigation by then. That morning in the conference room on the second floor of our offices on Harcourt Square, a team of about thirty-five detectives assembled to mount the operation. We had gathered all the data. I distributed our team into smaller crews, assigned them their locations and instructed them to arrest the suspects. And it was very fulfilling because it went like clockwork. Everyone was fully briefed and everyone did their job well on the day. It was all synchronised and co-ordinated efficiently and it was just one of those days when every cog in the machine worked perfectly in tandem together. We made nine arrests that day and brought them in for questioning; we followed up with raids on their homes.

We didn't have to go far to capture John Veldman. He was due to collect his cheque for April in Telecom's offices down the road that morning. And he duly turned to up collect it – this one was worth £18,489.95. And having signed for it, he then got a fair old shock. A couple of our detectives approached him, introduced themselves and told him he was under arrest. He was brought in for questioning. He didn't put up any resistance and made several admissions about his role in the fraud. And it turned out that the call cards he and his accomplices had been using were fabricated by Veldman himself. They were cloned cards. And they could be recharged so they could be used multiple times. All these thousands of phone calls they'd been making over the previous twelve months were free calls. Veldman had downloaded the information on how to do it online. He had bought a Microchip PicStart programmer to program the necessary software on his computer. He had bought computer chips and sheets of circuit board. And soon he had figured out how to manufacture call cards which could copy more or less exactly the official Telecom Éireann call card; they were compatible with Telecom's card phones in that they would activate the unit counter within the card phone once the call began. He first tested the clone card himself and when he was satisfied that it was working okay, he fabricated more of them and started to expand his network of accomplices to build profit. Each person he recruited would be given a card and, in addition, a PIN number. They would dial the 1580 number followed by the PIN and this would enable him to know on his computer which person was using which card. From that, he could register how many minutes they were clocking up and calculate how much he would have to pay them. A search of his business premises in the Edenmore shopping centre turned up several more cloned cards, the equipment he was using and computer printouts showing the revenue that each of his associates was generating, plus invoices, bank account statements and other documentation from the various accounts he'd set up to manage the money coming in and going out.

It turned out too that he had a lodger of sorts in his business premises, an associate who would bed down in the office at night. Ken Parkes was an alcoholic and suffered with epilepsy. He helped Veldman fix computers. He was arrested on the day and admitted he knew about the scam but claimed not to have made any of the bogus phone calls.

Two women were arrested that day. The courier whose papers we'd previously checked had three previous convictions for different offences but made no admission after being arrested and questioned, although we had observed him making calls to the 1580 number on Stephen's Green, Waterloo Road, Cuffe Street, Bride Street and Clanbrassil Street. The DCU student was arrested at his home in Glasnevin and he co-operated. He took down a box of cereal out of the press in his kitchen and fished a clone card out of it that was wrapped in kitchen roll. He told detectives that he'd met Veldman the previous autumn in a pub in Coolock, the Sheaf O'Wheat. Veldman offered him 'an easy but boring' way to make money. He would be paid 24p per minute of each call. He admitted making calls from kiosks on the Kilbarrack Road, outside the Botanic Gardens and near the Brian Boru pub in Glasnevin. He claimed he received about £1,000 in all from Veldman. He was studying computer applications in DCU and said he'd gotten involved in the scam to help pay his way through college. Another suspect had seven previous convictions. He'd been logged making calls outside Peats of Parnell Street and the Royal Dublin Hotel on O'Connell Street; at a kiosk on the junction of Talbot Street and Amiens Street, outside a fruit and veg shop in Fairview; on the Clonliffe Road, Poplar Road, the North Strand and the junction of Dorset Street and North Circular Road. Most of these were twin kiosks and in the booth next door was a friend of his, also engaged in the same scam, frequently at the same time. He too was arrested but, like his associate, did not make any admissions. Finally, there was a sergeant in the army who'd been observed making a call to the number from a kiosk on Leinster Road, Rathmines. He was arrested in Cathal Brugha Barracks.

While investigating the flow of money in and out of Netstar's accounts, it became obvious to us that AIB and Bank of Ireland should have flagged up what was going on here. Big cheques were being lodged and as soon as they cleared the accounts were rapidly being drained down to almost nil every month. And most of the money was being withdrawn in cash sums from ATMs on an almost daily basis. It wasn't normal activity. It was an irregular way for a business to manage its cash flow and general finances. It should have been classified as suspicious activity, possibly a money-laundering scheme, and someone in the relevant banking departments should have spotted these patterns. They weren't to know that the cash was being withdrawn to pay the runners in a fraud operation. But these were strange patterns and the banks should have notified the Garda Bureau of Fraud Investigation on the basis that there might be some sort of money-laundering exercise going on. If they had, it could have been nipped in the bud much earlier and we would have been going to Telecom about it rather than them coming to us.

This was one of these sprawling investigations with so many people and moving parts; it took us a long time to finally bring it all together. It was also believed to have been the first scam of its kind that had been perpetrated anywhere in Europe. We were moving into the electronic era of fraud, distinct from the old analogue era of pen and paper and handwritten forgeries and the like.

By the following summer we had completed our report. It took multiple volumes to contain it all. We handed it over to the Chief State Solicitor's office and from there it went to the DPP. One by one the cases against the runners came back with the recommendation that they should not be continued. Again there was the familiar story of us putting huge time and effort into making sure every i was dotted and every t was crossed, only to get an opinion back from the DPP that there was insufficient evidence, or some other reason that we couldn't fully understand.

Veldman and Parkes were brought forward for trial. They'd been remanded on continuing bail since their arrests. In May 2001 Veldman pleaded guilty to three counts of obtaining cheques under false pretences with intent to defraud Telecom Éireann; Parkes pleaded guilty to two charges. Parkes was described in court as 'a glorified messenger boy' while Veldman was described as 'the brains of the operation'. In June at the Dublin Circuit Criminal Court, Judge Yvonne Murphy handed Veldman a three-year suspended sentence. He was ordered to pay £40,000 back to Telecom Éireann over the next six years. Parkes got a two-year sentence, also suspended.

16

THE NIGERIAN MINISTRY OF WORKS AND HOUSING

You will have a fair idea that a fella is trying to hide something when he starts eating the evidence. Either that or the fella has worked up a desperate appetite altogether. And you wouldn't think there'd be much sustenance in a paper bank draft, even if it is written out to the tune of US$56.5 million. It's a lot of money but it's nearly all calories, you'd imagine.

Anyway, this particular chap, a Nigerian fraudster by the name of Christian Obumneme, decided to do exactly that when he and a few of his associates were intercepted by members of the Garda Fraud Squad on College Green in the spring of 1999. We had been on the trail of this particular gang for a number of weeks. They were operating out of an office on Baggot Street. With them that day was a German businessman who had travelled to Ireland on the promise of major money from this seemingly legitimate company. They were on their way in a taxi to the big Bank of Ireland branch on College Green where, *mar dhea*, they would lodge the $56.5 million draft and then hand the German his share. The taxi was intercepted by a couple of car loads of detectives and uniformed Gardaí. The suspects were ordered out of the taxi and as soon as Obumneme realised they were caught red-handed he stuffed the draft into his mouth and started chewing it to try and force it down his gullet. One of our lads, Det. Sgt Ronan Galligan, grabbed him and next thing they were grappling and wrestling on the ground. It was a pissing wet day, both of them were wearing full suits – I had to authorise costs to Ronan afterwards for the loss of his good suit!

It was worth every penny as it turned out. Obumneme put up ferocious resistance in the street. It took three guards to pin him to the pavement while Ronan tried to prise the document out from behind his clenched teeth. In fact, Obumneme only finally spat it out when they got him into Pearse Street station about half an hour later. It was smeared with blood and saliva. Five men in total were arrested and remanded in custody until the trial began at the Dublin Circuit Criminal Court in June 2000. At the trial, prosecuting counsel Patrick Gageby described said bank draft as 'a bit chewed but still discernible'. The evidence was intact. Det. Galligan had done the State some service that wet day on College Green. Indeed, you could say he had rescued victory from the jaws of defeat.

The company on Baggot Street was named World Wide Clearing and Finance (WWCF). Their business was fraud, and fraud on a grand scale, millions of dollars if they could pull in the suckers who'd fall for their scams.

One of their wheezes was to offer to recoup money on behalf of people who'd already been swindled, probably by accomplices and associates of WWCF. If they could be swindled once, maybe they could be swindled twice, like gamblers chasing their losses and desperate to salvage something from the next race. With an office, phone lines, computers and staff, WWCF looked, on the surface, like a legitimate operation. (The trial would hear from a regulator at the Central Bank that WWCF had never been registered as a finance company with the Central Bank, as it was required to do under law.) It was from this base that they went fishing all over Europe and further afield.

In this case, three Nigerians and two Caucasian males with London addresses were charged with fraud conspiracy involving over $143 million in forged bank drafts. The latter pair, being white and not having Nigerian accents, would have been important in terms of neutralising the suspicions of people who found themselves being offered amazing amounts of money by strangers. That was twenty years ago now, but this particular branch of the fraud industry already had a notorious international reputation. I have to say that in my time investigating fraud, Nigerian crooks kept coming up in the caseload. I don't know why, but that's the way it was. You'd hear the details of a particular banking or business or credit card scam and you'd know before even asking that there was a Nigerian angle to it. It got to the stage where it just wouldn't surprise you anymore. And it was also my experience that when you made contact with almost any Nigerian suspect, the first thing they'd do is play the race card. You were being racist, you were stereotyping them, etc. Basically, they were trying to make you feel guilty about it so that you might back off. But you saw through that particular tactic fairly early. Your job was to follow the money, as they say, and follow it without fear or favour.

WWCF first came to our attention through the American Secret Service. They had been alerted by a businessman from Baton Rouge, Louisiana. His name was Terry Smith, owner of the American Plumbing Company. Smith turned out to be a brilliant character in the witness box. When he was being cross-examined, he met fire with fire, sometimes with hilarious comments that no Irish person would say in a court of law. Whatever the defence barristers threw at him, he threw it back with interest.

Smith's evidence was that he'd first become embroiled in this scam when he was written to by a number of gentlemen claiming that they were officials from the Works and Housing Ministry of the Nigerian government. According to their story, a foreign construction company that had been building a massive housing project in Nigeria had gone bankrupt, leaving the job unfinished. So they had finished the job themselves and were entitled to $32 million from the government for so doing. But because they were government employees, they couldn't claim for it themselves. And this was where Mr Smith could be of great assistance to them. They would register his company as having completed the housing project and in return he would get $4 million. They would supply all the documentation needed to tick all the boxes from a bureaucratic point of view. His office in Baton Rouge duly received this documentation, including a fax purportedly from the Nigerian Ministry of Works and Housing confirming that the American Plumbing Company had paid income tax of over $100,000 for profits made between 1995 and 1997.

And now the Irish connection came into play. In another fax, this time on headed notepaper which read 'Nigerian Central Bank', he was notified that he would have to collect the $32 million draft through a Dublin-based company called World Wide Clearing and Finance. On 17 February 1999, Smith flew to Ireland. He made his way to the office on Baggot Street where he was introduced to various personnel, including a 'Richard Holborn', who later turned out to be Thomas O'Brien, one of the pair who had London addresses. Smith was also introduced to a chap called 'David Baker', which the prosecution alleged was a cover name for another of the accused. The next day they went to the Terenure branch of the Bank of Ireland. 'David Baker' went off for a little while and came back with a bank draft for the $32 million, made out to either Terry Smith or the American Plumbing Company, he couldn't remember which. They returned to the office on Baggot Street and this was where the worm turned. Smith was introduced to an auditor for WWCF, who told him there was a slight problem. The housing project back in Nigeria hadn't been completed. It would have to be completed before the relevant authorities would sign off on the $32 million payment. Therefore, if Smith could lodge $2 million with a designated bank account in

Nigeria to get the housing project completed, he would in due course get the $4 million promised to him. At this stage, Smith made his excuses and left. He said in evidence that he was never in danger of being defrauded because he never had any intention of handing over any money.

The trial judge was Pat McCartan, the former politician. Thomas O'Brien's lawyer was Martin Giblin SC. Cross-examining Smith, Giblin alleged the witness had been complicit in this enterprise, that he knew it was a 'bogus' scheme but had gone along with this attempt to 'hoodwink' the Nigerian government. Smith denied this, saying he'd had 'strong suspicions' about it from the start and had treated the correspondence over and back with WWCF as 'kind of a hobby'. In addition, his own attorney had warned him that other businessmen in Baton Rouge had received bogus offers from Nigeria. So he knew and understood from the start that this was a scam. Asked why then he had travelled to Dublin at all, Smith said one of his great-grandfathers originally hailed from Ireland and he wanted to see the country anyway. There was laughter from the public gallery when Giblin suggested to Smith that maybe he was also hoping to pick up a $32 million payment while checking out the home of his ancestors.

When Smith went back to the States after his encounter with WWCF, he alerted police authorities. He was put in touch with an agent from the Secret Service named Wayne Presley. The Secret Service in turn contacted the Garda Fraud Squad and Ronan Galligan was dispatched to Baton Rouge to meet Presley and interview Terry Smith. The three of them watched video stills of Smith and 'Richard

Holborn' and 'David Baker' entering the Bank of Ireland branch in Terenure that day.

It was ten or twelve days later when Ronan and the crew had their contretemps with Messrs Obumneme and O'Brien. The German businessman in their company that day was a software millionaire by the name of Heinz Althoff. Obumneme and O'Brien were arrested at the scene while the three others were arrested in follow-up swoops. Further investigations brought us to a house in Clonee in Meath where our members found a $40.2 million bank draft hidden behind a bedroom curtain and made out to a 'Jan Otto', and another draft with the exact same serial number made out to something called 'Plasondo Lda Lisboa'. In the hot press they found a South African passport and an ID card made out in the name of an 'Oscar Prince Naduka'. The passport and ID card each displayed a photo of Christian Obumneme. 'Oscar Prince Naduka' also had a provisional driving license.

Unlike Terry Smith, Mr Althoff had already been lured in and duped. He had parted with one million deutschmarks (about 400,000 Irish pounds) from his bank account in Frankfurt as an 'advance fee' to WWCF. They had promised him 10 per cent of the $56.5 million if he agreed to receive the transfer of this gigantic sum from a Nigerian bank account to his account. He told the trial he'd handed over the one million deutschmarks because he feared for his life. 'You can hire the Russian mafia for only $2,000,' he said. I'd imagine that witnessing the altercation on College Green that day didn't do much to calm his fears.

Midway through the trial, one of the five accused was cleared of all charges by Judge McCartan due to insufficient evidence. Various defence lawyers put us through the ringer. One of them addressed McCartan saying that the handling of the exhibits in this case was corrupt and that we were concocting lies and all sorts. It was terrible having to sit there and listen to it. I was a superintendent by then and in that capacity had given permission to have the suspects' fingerprints taken and to have their time in custody extended until the trial came round. I was in the witness box giving evidence when this genius of a barrister decided to go into a long spiel about the discrimination and falsehoods that were spreading all over the world about Nigerian citizens. It was basically an attempt to taint the evidence we were giving. So at the end of his spiel, I turned to McCartan and apologised and said I didn't understand the question. Could the barrister repeat it please? And off he went on another long-winded spiel about the hardship and poverty in Nigerian society, and had I discussed this with Det. Galligan when we were investigating the case? And at the end of this performance I just said, 'No. I didn't discuss it with him.' I wouldn't elaborate any further, just left the lawyer hanging there. There was a long pause and I could see he was livid with my answer. But I happened to catch a glimpse of Judge McCartan and there he was smiling away to himself in his chair.

Witnesses from the Companies Office gave evidence that WWCF had been set up by directors using fictitious names and address. Accomplices in Nigeria had contacted many businessmen around the world and told them they could make tens of millions of dollars by allowing massive dollar transfers into their bank accounts. When the businessmen came to Ireland, they were told that they would have to pay millions of dollars first before receiving the payments into their accounts. Payments which, of course, would never materialise, as poor Mr Althoff discovered.

The court proceedings lasted twenty-four days. The jury found three of the accused guilty of various fraud offences. Judge McCartan jailed O'Brien for five years. His fellow London addressee, Raymond Folkes, got four years. Christian Obumneme also got four years. He was living in Stoneybatter, Dublin 7, and was applying for refugee status in Ireland at the time. As I recall he served his jail sentence and was subsequently deported. The fifth accused was cleared of all charges by the jury. The fella was elated. He burst into tears and started shouting 'Hallelujah!' over and over.

We were pretty happy too, overall, because it was a landmark case. It was the first time in the history of the State that a case of this nature had been successfully prosecuted. It was the first time that a fraud ring had been caught operating out of its headquarters and it was the first time that this particular strain of scam, the so-called 'advance fee fraud', had been encountered in western Europe. It was also unique in that the operation was not aimed at Irish people but at foreigners who would be lured to Ireland by what seemed like a legitimately registered company. We estimated that up to fifty foreigners had dealings with WWCF in the four weeks of February/ March 1999 alone. What I said at the time remains as true now as it was then: 'What should be learned from this is that if it sounds too good to be true, then it isn't true.'

But not everyone who gets caught up in scams is an innocent party. A lot of people who end up tangled in these webs are themselves involved in dodgy dealings. They will have obtained money illegally and want to find some way of laundering it, maybe to be able to claim that the money in their account was put there by Nigerian scam merchants. Or they will want to hide their ill-gotten gains by investing in a proposition that they know is illegal but they hope will yield a quick return and maybe give them cover.

Still and all, you'd be amazed too at the amount of ordinary people who can't or won't see the flashing red lights. The prospect of handy money seems to override their common sense. Greed blinds them to all the warning signs. You wouldn't have this enormous fraud problem worldwide if enough people weren't tempted by the lure of free money. To be fair, sometimes it's not greed but desperation that brings people to this sorry pass. The Nigerian fraud industry has evolved to the point that they have the financial acumen to identify businesses that are struggling and home in on them. If the business owner is in deep enough trouble, he or she may be tempted to try one of these arrangements in a last-ditch effort to save the company. These people aren't blinded by greed; in fact, they're very vulnerable. And if they end up getting swindled in these circumstances it can tip them over the edge.

We all know of stories of the aftermath of the Celtic Tiger crash, where, tragically, some businessmen who went bankrupt took their own lives. Now imagine the anguish and distress if you've been struggling to keep your business above water for a couple of years and your last cash reserves have been robbed by conmen? And you helped them do it? Many victims of fraud have taken their own lives. I know of a farmer in Cavan who lost his holding of land as a result of handing over money to Nigerian fraudsters. He lost all his money; he could no longer pay back the mortgage he had on the land and the bank moved in to reclaim the farm. That man died by suicide. The fraud industry preys upon people who are in trouble as well as people who are greedy or people who are incredibly naive. It wouldn't exist if there weren't so many frailties and vulnerabilities in human beings. Senior citizens are often targeted too.

In Ireland there were Nigerian fraud rings operating from the early 1990s at least. And with the aforementioned Celtic Tiger taking off, more of them arrived to avail of the rich pickings. Millions of scamming letters are sent all over the world every year and now Irish people were getting letters that were promising more pots of gold than a leprechaun at the end of the rainbow. These letters would be signed by a 'government official', the 'private secretary to the President of Nigeria' and the 'Financial Controller of the Nigerian National Petroleum Corporation'.

In 1998 we came across a scam known as 'black money'. Two suitcases of black money were discovered in Clonee, Co. Meath. What happens in this scenario is that the patsy is shown a suitcase of what are supposed to be bank notes, often $100 notes, that have been camouflaged with a black chemical dye. The fairy tale they spin is that the money had to be disguised to smuggle it out of Nigeria. But, and this is the big but, they have another chemical that can clean the black stuff off the currency. Then they'll give you a demonstration. They'll take a hundred-dollar bill, let's say, that is completely blacked out and apply the chemical to it and hey presto, magic! You have a spanking fresh hundred-dollar bill in front of you. They are literally laundering the money in this particular swindle. And there's a suitcase there packed with blacked-out dollar bills, waiting to be transformed into perfect greenbacks. All you have to do is pay for the chemical agent that will transform the notes from black to green. There's a million dollars in that suitcase so we'll charge you a 10 per cent cut for the chemical and the cash – $100,000 and it's all yours. Now, naturally enough, even a total eejit will want to take a brick of the 'cash' in his hands and feel the weight of it and inspect the goods. But they have an answer for that too: the suitcase can only be opened for a few seconds because the black dye will react to air and destroy the money. But, as Ronan Galligan said at the time, 'all you're ever left with is a substance that usually explodes in your fridge and a case full of black paper'.

While we were investigating our case, we liaised from time to time with the London Metropolitan Police. The London Met had a fully dedicated Nigerian scam investigation unit in their fraud bureau. They were full-time on the trail of these cons and conmen and were familiar with some of the names in our investigation. They could even recognise suspects by their voices on the phone.

Along with the British, the Americans were also taking a keen interest in the progress of the case in Dublin. We had liaised with the Secret Service before on a different case. They had been tracking a con job in America involving the wife of a very rich businessman. They had bugged the phones and were taping the conversations between her and her new Nigerian friends who were, as usual, offering a fortune. It turned out that these chaps were based in Ireland. When the Feds in America discovered that she was going to come to Ireland and hand over a bank draft for a very large sum of money, they tipped us off. They had the details of her itinerary; she was flying in to Dublin airport on a given day and she would be meeting her partners in this new venture at the Burlington Hotel. We trailed her from the airport to the hotel. She went up to the reception; we were looking round to see if there were any Nigerian businessmen in the lobby. After a few minutes waiting we went up to her and introduced ourselves. Next thing we saw this black chap running for the door. A few of our men were outside; they caught him and arrested him. The woman got an awful shock. She couldn't believe it when we told her who we were, why we were there and the involvement of the Secret Service. She said she had a bank draft in her luggage that she was going to lodge into the businessmen's account; they were going to meet her at the Burlington and take her to a branch of the bank they used. Interestingly, she said what swayed her towards believing it was a genuine business opportunity was the fact that the company in question was based in Ireland. She thought because the transaction was taking place in Ireland, we wouldn't have fraud here, it would all be above board. The poor lady was distraught. We brought the Nigerian chap in for questioning, but of course he denied everything and we didn't have enough on him to charge him with anything.

We had also been liaising with the Secret Service over the WWCF case on an ongoing basis. The last day or two of the trial was attended by one of their top officers. Mike Stenger specialised in financial crime, cyber crime and fraud. We had a sit-down with Mike after the case was over. He had been sent over because the American authorities had been combating this kind of crime for over twenty years. They had seen it expand and evolve into a massive, multi-million-dollar racket. And apparently, we were the first police force that had managed to secure convictions against Nigerian fraudsters anywhere in the world. As a result, Mike invited Galligan and myself to speak at a conference in the States on Nigerian organised crime. Needless to say, we were delighted to take him up on the offer.

The conference was in Fort Lauderdale, Florida, in August 2000. It was put together by an organisation called the International Association of Financial Crimes Investigators. We had a fantastic week; we were given the VIP treatment from the moment we arrived. We had loads of high-ranking detectives and police officers coming up to us and congratulating us on our success. It was a big deal to them that a police force had managed to secure convictions against a fraud ring, maybe because they understood how difficult and complex it is to bring an investigation of that nature to a successful conclusion. And to emphasise the esteem in which they held the achievement, they presented Ronan with their Detective of the Year award. I was gifted a lovely plaque by the organisers which I still have at home, etched with the words: 'Presented by the United States Secret Service'.

At the conference I introduced the background to the story and Ronan talked them through the nuts and bolts of the operation, from day one to the day the suspects were jailed. I have given many a talk over the years at various conferences and to the banking and insurance industries and so forth, but I have to say it was hard to beat doing it in Florida. There were five hundred law enforcement personnel there that weekend and you got a clear idea of the sheer scale of the organised crime that is international fraud.

We attended a lot of the presentations made at the conference over its four days. An English police detective told the story of how he'd been involved in an operation that brought the investigators to Nigeria. They raided this enormous warehouse and it was wall-to-wall with people writing scam letters, sending faxes and making phone calls. I have no idea where they got all these addresses and phone numbers and fax numbers from, but they had them and they were peppering businesses and citizens all over the world with their financial tall tales. The whole thing was an eye-opener for this English detective.

But it's funny the things you remember. One thing that stands out for me was our stopover in Washington DC on the way home. There was an Irish bar and restaurant just across the road from the Secret Service headquarters there called Fadó which was popular with the local law enforcement personnel and which they pronounced as 'Faydo'. We were wined and dined royally in 'Faydo' that evening.

In Fort Lauderdale we had two Secret Service fellas who were sort of our guides and minders for the week. They were gas men altogether, mad into their golfing, so they took us to a course for eighteen holes on one of the days. I remember distinctly Ronan taking a swing at a ball and making a hash of it. And as frustrated golfers often do, he let out a swear at himself. 'Ah you effin' bollocks!' The pair of Americans cracked up with the laughing. They'd never heard the expression before and were asking us what it meant. And for the rest of the day, they couldn't stop saying it and cracking up all over again.

When we got back to Ireland we were still basking in the glow of Florida and the acclaim and the good times we had there in glorious sunshine. The Garda Commissioner and the Assistant Commissioner of the Crime Branch had also sent us letters of commendation. But of course, the basking didn't last that long. Soon enough you were back to the wind and the rain, and back to dealing with the usual array of conmen and liars and gougers of every description. In other words, there was no shortage of effin' bollockses to be dealing with when we got home.

17

TAYLOR'S ASSETS

Detective Garda Kevin Monks had been on the trail of Tony Taylor for three years. Taylor was an investment broker who had absconded from Dublin in August 1996, leaving a trail of defrauded clients in his wake. It would become what was then the largest investigation in Fraud Squad history – or the Garda Bureau of Fraud Investigation (GBFI) as we were now formally known. I entrusted it to a team of detectives led by Det. Sgt Gerry Walsh with Det. Garda Kevin Monks at the forefront, one of our most experienced and determined investigators. Kevin got onto it and basically didn't stop until Taylor ended up behind bars.

In the following months and years, we heard several tip-offs and rumours about his whereabouts, but they were dead ends. We eventually traced him to the seaside town of Eastbourne, about twenty miles from Brighton on the south coast of England. He had set himself up in a finance business again, operating under the name of 'Andrew' Taylor. He was conducting electronic transactions through the Channel Islands and it all led back to a residential address in Eastbourne. By then we had built up a dossier of files on his complicated wheeling and dealing with other people's money. Once we knew where he was living, we requested the police authorities in England to place his house under surveillance while we finalised our documentation and submitted it to the DPP. It had been an incredibly complex, hugely time-consuming investigation. We had to gather information from financial institutions in the UK, Jersey, the Isle of Man and Luxembourg, all of which involved the elaborate process of making applications to the courts in those jurisdictions. Pulling it all together was a big job of work so once he finally surfaced, we were determined to get him into a court of law to face the music. We drafted a ream of warrants for his arrest on a list of charges and an extradition application to bring him back to Ireland. Paperwork completed, Monks and myself took a flight to London and from there, travelled to Eastbourne. It was 11 August 1999, and I remember the date because it was the day of the total solar eclipse, which caused a huge amount of excitement at the time.

We teamed up with local police and officers from their National Crime Squad. They would execute the arrest warrants. We then went to Taylor's house on a road called Wrestwood Avenue. It was a comfortable suburban house in a well-to-do neighbourhood in a town that was a popular retreat for the retired middle classes. The lead British officer knocks on the door; the man himself answers. 'Are you Anthony Taylor?' He nodded; he was speechless for a few moments. The officer told him who we were, showed him the warrants for his arrest and informed him we had an extradition warrant to bring him back to Ireland to face these charges.

The officer asked if we could come in; he stepped back and let us through. The first thing I noticed was a set of golf clubs and a pair of golf shoes in the hallway. I knew he loved his golf, as did I, so I got talking to him about that, just to establish a bit of a rapport. It's far easier on everyone involved if you can be civil in these situations and avoid being confrontational in word or deed. He told me he was a member of a local golf club and played there regularly. I remember asking him what his handicap was and him replying that his game had deteriorated due to the fact that everyone was calling him 'Andrew' and he couldn't get used to it. It made him feel uncomfortable playing under a different name. A lot of golfers come up with all sorts of reasons when they're fluffing their shots, but that was a new one on me.

Shirley, Taylor's second wife, was inside in the front lounge. The poor woman was in an absolute state of shock when she realised what was happening. Taylor was arrested and brought to a police station where he was remanded in custody overnight. The next day he was brought to Brighton Magistrates Court where I briefly gave evidence to confirm the existence of the warrants for his arrest back in Ireland. The judge granted our extradition order and remanded Taylor in custody pending an appeal against the order. His barrister said he would contest the order. I thought it was a bad move and I told Taylor as much in a private conversation. I was getting on well with him at this stage; you weren't dealing here with the sort of fella that Jim Brannigan was throwing into the back of a van every night, although he caused far more hurt and distress to people than most of those latchicos ever did. Taylor was a well-spoken, well-educated, courteous kind of liar and conman. I got on fine with him for the purposes of the business at hand. As I recall, I told him it was a pointless exercise trying to fight the extradition warrant. What's more, the British police had told him and me that if he did decide to fight it, he'd be kept in a prison for the duration where he was likely to get all sorts of abuse from inmates who'd take an instant dislike to him because he was the posh sort – and because he was Irish to boot. But he decided to go the legal route and ended up spending the next five months and more in jail, including Lewes prison. Eventually, after a lot of toing and froing with his legal team, the penny dropped; he couldn't outrun the extradition process.

On 28 January 2000, Kevin Monks and Det. Sgt Gerry Walsh flew to Gatwick Airport where Taylor was handed into their custody by British police and taken on the next flight back to Dublin. I met them at the airport, we brought him directly to Bridewell garda station and then to the District Court where the charges against him were read out.

Bear in mind that Taylor had been the proverbial pillar of society up until the roof caved in on him. He'd lived in a five-bedroom house called 'Somerset' on Anglesea Road, Ballsbridge, one of the best addresses in Dublin. The house was repossessed in his absence and sold for over half a million pounds. Husband and wife had been driving a top-of-the-range Mercedes and BMW. His offices were on Clyde Road, Ballsbridge.

In the second week of August '96 he was contacted by an inspector from the Department of Enterprise and Employment (DEE) informing him that some of his clients had registered formal complaints against him. The day before he was due to meet this inspector, Taylor ordered an employee to delete a raft of business names from the company's computer system. She was also told to start shredding documents. She filled some twenty black plastic bin bags with shredded material. The next day he met the inspector. They agreed to a further meeting a couple of days later, but Taylor never showed. He sold his Mercedes, his wife's BMW and they abandoned 'Somerset'. They left their beloved dog Harvey in the care of a staff member. We were brought in to investigate and a company liquidator was appointed. Shortly after he absconded, he wrote a letter to his solicitor saying, 'I am not running from the problem and will of course be available to answer any questions. In light of the media attention I feel that the best thing I now do is lie low for a short time while the DEE get on with their work.' And that was the last we heard from him for the next three years.

But in his glory days he'd been a former chairman of the Irish Brokers' Association. His company Taylor Asset Management was one of the biggest private managers of client funds outside of the financial institutions. He was running a group of companies which in total had some 1,200 clients and over £30 million in investments.

So he was a big player, a man about town, one of the most prominent in the Dublin investment community. He'd even been an advisor to senior civil servants as they drafted a comprehensive set of regulations that would eventually become the Investment Intermediaries Act of 1995. This was a badly overdue piece of legislation introduced to protect investors and impose a code of conduct, a set of rules and guidelines, on persons offering investment services to clients. And having thrown in his tuppence worth on the rules and regulations required, Taylor proceeded to break a fair few of them himself. In fact, he would be the first person to face a charge under the laws laid out in the Investment Intermediaries Act.

In the District Court that day he was charged with fraudulent conversion, forgery, obtaining money under false pretences and other offences. In financial terms it came to over £600,000 of other people's money. In reality, it was much more than that because some of his clients were trying to hide their money through his investment schemes and did not want to be exposed, for tax reasons or otherwise. They took their losses in secrecy. It was estimated that £1.7 million had gone missing. Taylor privately admitted that he'd moved millions of pounds offshore for wealthy clients but declined to name them. He complained bitterly that banks and other financial institutions were doing the same thing but he was the one who got caught.

Despite repeated applications for bail in the year that followed, Taylor remained in custody. He was in Cloverhill Prison on the day his son Paul, a financial consultant, got married in Dalkey in July 2001. Paul visited him in Cloverhill on the morning of the wedding. Taylor was still adamant at this stage that he would defend himself against all charges when the trial came round. But a full trial did not go ahead. On 2 October 2001, he pleaded guilty to a number of charges at the Dublin Circuit Criminal Court and was sentenced to five years in prison. He pleaded guilty to three counts of the fraudulent conversion of cheques, one count of the fraudulent diversion of funds for his own use, and to one count of the destruction of records and documents relating to Taylor Asset Management. Several other charges were dropped.

We reckoned that at least seventeen personal investors got burned. Taylor had been a prominent member of the Grange Golf Club in Rathfarnham. His connections here alone brought him a lot of business when he'd been building his client base through the 1970s and 1980s. At his peak, his reputation went before him as a man with the Midas touch when it came to dividends on investments. The word was that he was outperforming the big financial institutions and he wasn't shy about polishing the legend himself. Among his victims was a retired lady who'd handed him a cheque for £50,000 in 1991 and never saw a penny of it again. There was a man who lost over £150,000, an elderly gentleman who lost £136,000 and another woman who lost £31,000. Any time they asked how their investment was doing, he basically fobbed them off with a pack of lies. One of his tactics was to forge clients' signatures on the back of their cheques and then lodge the cheques to one or other of his many accounts.

Among the charges that were withdrawn was one concerning the Society of St Vincent de Paul and their Sunshine Fund. They lost £185,000. It was part of a bequest of £500,000 which the society had received from a donor. This donor had requested that a substantial chunk of the money should go towards the modernisation of Sunshine House in Balbriggan, a facility that provided summer holidays for children from disadvantaged backgrounds. The society intended to build an indoor play centre at Sunshine House which the children could enjoy when it was raining outside. Taylor had made a personal presentation to the people who managed the Sunshine House fund, seeking some of their money. They handed him over the £185,000, which again never saw the light of day. As part of his guilty plea strategy, Taylor wanted this particular charge dropped. He did not want it said that he had robbed £185,000 that had been earmarked for the benefit of children in need. And St Vincent de Paul were happy enough to see the charge disappear too. They didn't want the publicity either. It was very embarrassing for them to have lost a huge sum of money in this way. It tarnished their reputation as safe custodians of donated money. They ran a huge fundraising operation and something like this damaged the all-important principle of public trust.

Taylor's legal team argued in court that he hadn't used the vanished monies for personal expenditure but to shore up his failing companies. One of his lawyers explained that he'd suffered from a 'blindness to reality' when the business he had built up started to haemorrhage money. But it didn't disguise the fact that Taylor had a big ego and a prestigious reputation around the leafier parts of Dublin which he wanted to protect at all costs, or that he indulged in some very expensive tastes when it came to his lifestyle. He held onto the Mercedes and the BMW long after the business started to bleed. Plus, he paid himself very generously for the job of managing other people's money. Judge Elizabeth Dunne came down hard on him; five years for fraud offences was considered severe at the time. We had spent five years trying to track him down and assemble the case against him, at great cost to the State in terms of time, budget and manpower. We had lined up about sixty witnesses for the trial; we had tens of thousands of documents and thousands of exhibits prepared to be used in evidence. It had been a massive undertaking. For us it was a landmark prosecution in terms of proving our capacity to pursue a case of this complexity and magnitude. The Garda Bureau of Fraud Investigation had come a long way from the early days of the old Fraud Squad. We were much better resourced by then; we had more technical and financial expertise across the board – but we were still a long way short of what they would have today. A lot of it still came down to the dogged determination and professionalism of officers like Detectives Walsh and Monks.

When Judge Dunne delivered the sentence, Taylor stood there white in the face. He looked absolutely wretched. He had no friends or family members with him. As he was being led away in handcuffs, he nodded to myself and Monks. I nodded back. He disappeared through a door and was brought to Arbour Hill Prison. He had already spent more than two years on remand. Over the next nineteen months he would spend time in Arbour Hill, Cloverhill and the Mountjoy training unit. He was released in May 2003. He gave a couple of newspaper interviews in the following years. In one of them he seemed to be in denial that he had done anything wrong at all. He talked about how he was going to appeal the conviction in the Supreme Court and take it to the European courts then if necessary. Nothing ever happened in this regard. In another interview he said the prison experience wasn't as frightening as he thought it would be. 'I spent a lot of time in the gym,' he said. 'The food,' he added, 'wasn't too bad.'

18

THE GALWAY RACES

The mobile phone rang on my desk. It was Chief Superintendent Tom Monaghan. He had an unusual question. 'Are you at the Galway Races?'

Said I, 'I wish I was.' It was the end of July 2001 and it was a glorious evening. But I was chained to my desk in Harcourt Square, ploughing through a mound of correspondence. It was a far cry from the craic in Ballybrit.

'Why are you asking?'

'Because,' he replied, 'there's a fella down here claiming to be Superintendent Willie McGee, that's why.'

Tom was head of the Galway division; the races in Ballybrit would have been a big policing operation every year. It was the first day of the festival and he'd called into their offices on course that evening as a matter of courtesy. And there, the office manager told him a little story that strictly speaking she shouldn't be telling at all, because another senior Garda, a superintendent, had called to the office earlier that day, albeit in plain clothes and under the strictest confidence. In fact, he had phoned her some hours before and introduced himself as Supt Willie

McGee, head of the Fraud Squad in Dublin. He said he was investigating a scam that would be unfolding at the races. He and a colleague, a detective inspector, would need two passes, access all areas, for the week. (The festival would be running every day, up to and including the following Sunday.) It was an undercover operation so it was very important that she did not divulge their presence to anyone, not even the Galway Gardaí. He sounded plausible, and with so much cash floating around the betting ring and everywhere else, it sounded credible that there could be some sort of criminal carry-on going down. Later that day he called into the office, introduced himself in person and re-emphasised the importance of telling nobody. She handed him two badges and off he went.

It was an evening card. When Tom Monaghan heard the yarn, he smelled a rat immediately. He knew fine well there was no way the Fraud Squad would be landing down in Galway without clearing it with him first, as a matter of protocol and courtesy. And that was when he put the call into me back in Dublin. My first thought was that this was a stroke pulled by a professional fraudster whom I'd crossed swords with over the years and who was looking to pull a fast one just for the satisfaction of getting one over on me. Some of them actually thought like that: even if there wasn't much in it for themselves, they'd enjoy trying to embarrass you or making you the butt of a joke. But I was in for a surprise when the culprit was nabbed – we all were.

Crucially, the office manager hadn't given him his two passes for the week. She'd given him a pair for that day only. The arrangement was that he'd call into the office each morning and collect a pair of daily badges. The impostor duly turned up in the office the next day and was duly apprehended. It turned out he was a former Garda, one John Cunningham, originally from Boyle but living in Ballymote at the time. What's more, he'd been a classmate of mine in Templemore, the class of November '66. I hadn't come across him in the thirty-four years since we'd graduated; he'd been posted to stations down the country as far as I could recall.

But I had good reason for remembering him. Cunningham had done a stint in England working on the sites and was that bit more battle-hardened than the rest of us raw recruits who were a few years younger and had arrived straight from home. He fancied himself as a bit of a hard man in Templemore and seemed to think that the likes of myself was just a country gobshite with no experience of the real world. He got into the habit of taunting a few of us and belittling us with his smart remarks. And he seemed to pick on me a bit more often, maybe because I was so tall and skinny and stood out from the crowd. And I reckon because I was so gangly, he thought I'd be easy prey for a bit of bullying and pushing around. Anyway, the picking went on a bit too long for my liking and one day I decided to put it up to him. We had words and the words got more heated and it ended up with me hitting him a slap across the face with my open hand and inviting him to sort it out here and now. And just like that, he backed down; he mouthed something more and just slipped away. A crowd of the lads had gathered round to see this commotion and he got an awful slagging from them; they were openly calling him a coward and a bully boy. So what does our friend do? He goes whingeing to our class sergeant, Sgt O'Donovan, who was a very level-headed individual. He gave us a lecture, told us that we were training to be members of a disciplined, well-behaved organisation and if we didn't sort it out here and now, the matter would be going up the line to the training officer. And this chap would be taking a very dim view of our behaviour – we could be walking out the gate and going home. So, he convinced us to shake hands and move on. We very reluctantly shook hands and then avoided each other like the plague for the remainder of the course.

Our paths never crossed again once we left the training college in the spring of '67. And now here he appears out of the mists of time, arrested for impersonating me. Were the two things linked? Was it his way of thinking he'd have the last laugh? If it was, it was a fairly sad way to be thinking.

Cunningham had retired from the force by then. His 'colleague' on this top-secret assignment in Ballybrit, the so-called detective inspector, was still a serving member. He was also from Boyle. He'd been spotted outside the office waiting for Cunningham to come out with the badges. But as soon as he saw Gardaí congregating around the office, he did a runner and disappeared off the course. Cunningham wouldn't identify him under questioning and we knew if we brought him in, he'd deny everything and we wouldn't have the proof to make it stand up in court. But he was as guilty as the impostor. And in general, he was known within the force as being dodgy, not to be trusted. I'd known him for years in the job.

You might wonder why they bothered trying to pull this stunt in the first place. It was such a small sort of petty stroke to be pulling. To save themselves the price of the admission fee? Impersonating a Garda was a risky thing to be doing for such modest financial savings. I think it was more to do with ego. They wanted to be big shots. They wanted to be swanning about the place with their badges on, getting into the VIP section and the parade ring and the winners' enclosure; Cunningham would've loved to be seen backslapping the winning jockeys and trainers and shaking hands with them and generally gatecrashing the show.

He was arrested that morning and taken to one of the stations in the city. He admitted everything straightaway; he couldn't do anything else; he'd been caught red-handed. The next question was, had he pulled the same scam at the Curragh, Fairyhouse, Leopardstown, Punchestown, Listowel and so on? I rang them one by one; they all came back negative. They couldn't recall anything like that ever happening. But in my opinion, even if they could, they'd have been too embarrassed to tell me.

Cunningham was charged with impersonating a member of An Garda Síochána and obtaining credit by fraud. He was brought before Judge John Garavan at the Galway District Court, but I wasn't involved in the prosecution of the case and wasn't there on the day. The first I knew about it was when I read it in the *Connacht Tribune*. His solicitor told the court that his client had retired in 1996 after thirty years of 'exemplary' service.

In actual fact, he'd been in disciplinary trouble a number of times during his career. His solicitor also said that Cunningham had apologised to me. But he hadn't; he never contacted me at all. I don't know how that assertion was let pass without the prosecuting superintendent picking him up on it. It was false information. In the end, Judge Garavan fined him £200 and Cunningham, I presume, went back to Ballymote with his tail between his legs.

And then of course, Ireland being a small country, didn't I bump into him only a few years ago in the Orchard Restaurant in Celbridge. He came over to me to make small talk; how's things, how's the family, the usual ould guff when you're talking to someone you don't want to be talking to. But as we were parting, I couldn't resist firing a shot. It came to me in a flash and I asked it in a flash: 'Do you still go to the Galway races?' Well Jesus, the look on his face. He stopped dead in his tracks. I'd have loved to have someone beside me to see the look on his face – it was priceless. He stuttered out some reply and shuffled off with himself.

In 2016 we, the class of November '66, had our fiftieth anniversary reunion. He could have apologised to me there, I suppose. And I could have told him in no uncertain terms that there was only one Willie McGee. But for some reason or another, he didn't turn up.

19

END OF THE LINE

In August 2002 I handed in my badge and gun. The time had come to saddle up my horse and ride off into the sunset.

I had gone into Templemore in the autumn of 1966, a fairly raw and innocent country boy. Now I was fifty-five and neither raw nor innocent anymore. It would've taken a lot to shock me by that stage. You couldn't spend nearly thirty-six years in the police force and not see a lot of the worst in human nature. Sometimes you saw the best of it too. And in between the best and the worst there was the whole spectrum of human behaviour in all its strangeness and unpredictability and strength and vulnerability.

I had become steeped in the ways of An Garda Síochána, one of the most important institutions in Irish society. I worked with some outstanding professionals and many good people who tried to bring a bit of humanity to their work as well as sound judgement and conscientious enforcement of the law. I worked with some awful eejits too and came across a few too many bad apples. Just as in society, there was quite the spectrum of human life in the police force as well.

In later years my work environment changed considerably as the organisation in general continued to evolve and modernise. The world of fraud had changed massively from the days when you had a few fellas at the back of a shop slicing strips off £20 notes and putting the strips together like a jigsaw with a bit of sellotape to form a new £20 note! Those fellas were artists! It was a whole different ball game now.

There was general consensus at official levels that fraud detection needed to be overhauled. The computer revolution meant that big-time financial fraud was starting to exploit the new technology too. A review body in the early 1990s recommended that the Fraud Squad should be headed up by a detective superintendent. Fachtna Murphy went into that role. In 1993/94 a major review was commissioned, chaired by senior counsel Peter Maguire and including civil servants from the finance and justice departments, an accountant from KPMG and a chief superintendent, Frank Glacken. They went on fact-finding missions to Canada and the UK. Their report had a raft of recommendations, including the recruitment of Gardaí with legal and accounting qualifications, a chief superintendent to lead the unit and a change of name to the Garda Bureau of Fraud Investigation (GBFI). The chief super would be designated Director of the Bureau, a superintendent would be Deputy Director. I was appointed to the latter post in February '96. Fachtna was promoted to chief super but moved to another division. Frank Glacken was the first director of the new GBFI but because he hadn't specialised in fraud during his career,

Frank's role was more managerial. I headed up many of the live investigations and was hands-on in the day-to-day running of the staff, which now numbered about eighty. It was an extremely busy and rewarding time in my career. I'd like to think I had a good working relationship with everyone who reported to me. I tried not to be rank-conscious. I preferred to be addressed by my first name, I was on first-name terms with all my staff. We worked well together I think. I'm happy to be able to say that I mentored quite a few young Gardaí there who went on to have fine careers in the force. I took great pride in seeing them progress through the ranks and in time become superintendents and chief superintendents themselves.

On top of keeping tabs on the major investigations going on, I was knee-deep in the administrative end of things too. The work involved travelling to international conferences on fraud, including regular meetings in Brussels during the years when planning for the introduction of the Euro currency were advancing. Obviously that was an enormous undertaking at the time and one of the issues they had to plan for was counterfeiting, which was where fraud officers from all over Europe were brought in as part of a counter-strategy.

It was actually far too big a workload for one man. The revamped model hadn't solved every problem. The increase in personnel and the greater number of investigations meant more and more paperwork was landing on my desk. I myself had been agitating for substantial change over the years, both in the legislation and in the resources we had at our disposal. We needed specialist personnel such as forensic accountants and lawyers, and we got them, but we also needed a second superintendent to take up some of the workload. One to head up the investigations, the other to head up the administration. There was a constant stream of investigation files coming through the system. These had to be carefully read and scrutinised; you'd be back and forth to your officers with all sorts of follow-up questions; you had to make sure every i was dotted and every t was crossed before they were passed onto the State Solicitor's office. You'd have staff coming to you all the time looking for advice on different aspects of the investigations they were conducting. Or they'd be looking for you to make applications for court orders and the like. Many of these investigations would be complex, highly detailed, hugely time-consuming. Your phone would be ringing from morning to evening.

By the turn of the millennium I knew my time in Garda fraud was drawing to a close. But I would only be in my mid-fifties by then and I wasn't near ready to retire to my garden and smell the roses. I was fit, I was healthy, I wanted to work. And I knew there would be opportunities in the corporate sector for somebody with my knowledge and experience. The banking and insurance industries were haunted by the spectre of fraud and I heard on the grapevine that both AXA Insurance and Ulster Bank were looking to beef up their security operations in this regard. Both of them offered me contracts, on the same day as it happened, and with suitably attractive terms and conditions. AXA's offer appealed to me more because the expertise they required was more directly related to my own working life. They were setting up a new fraud investigations unit and they wanted me to be part of it. So I accepted their offer.

In August 2002 I retired from the force. And I wasn't gone six months when they appointed a second superintendent and split the roles between investigations and administration. I had a big retirement do at the Garda sports and leisure centre in Westmanstown with well over three hundred people there on the night. Pat Byrne was the Garda Commissioner at the time and he spoke at it. It was a wonderful occasion. Old colleagues and friends turned up in huge numbers, a lot of craic was had and a lot of stories were told. That night brought the curtain down on my life in blue. The next day was the first day of the rest of my life.

20

PASTURES NEW

In September 2002 I began my new career. In terms of recruitment and resources, AXA were going to a great deal of cost in setting up a new investigations unit. Within a few years they were making it back, and multiples along with it, because of the frauds detected and prevented and the money saved that would otherwise have been paid out for bogus claims. In fact, I would go so far as to say that I never realised how widespread insurance fraud was, or just how many dishonest people were out there, until I started working in this new role. The insurance companies were seen almost as a legitimate target for swindling money by far more people than I ever imagined.

John O'Neill was the CEO of AXA at the time. The company had commissioned a survey of 1,200 people about their attitude to insurance fraud. It found that 51 per cent of the respondents said they would make a dishonest claim if they thought they could get away with it. Four out of ten said they believed fraud was common in making insurance claims; 64 per cent agreed that most people inflate the value of their claim by at least one third. On the other hand, and there seemed to be a bit of doublethink going on here, 75 per cent agreed that insurance companies should prosecute dishonest claimants.

The findings alarmed O'Neill and senior management; they were similar to surveys in the US and UK where insurance fraud was now being dubbed 'the crime of the '90s'. It was becoming widespread and the big insurers in America and Britain had responded by setting up their own internal Special Investigation Units (SIUs). AXA were the first to do likewise in Ireland. The unit would have four personnel: a general manager, myself as the fraud investigations manager, an accountant and an experienced claims handler. The unit had a red flag system in place to help staff identify any circumstances that were unusual in nature or that varied in some way from normal conventions.

I wasn't a month in the job when we had our first scam hooked. A woman had taken out a fully comprehensive insurance policy on a 2002 Nissan Primera, a brand-new car, in September. She was a member of the travelling community, a Ms McDonagh. In October she rang the office and reported that her car had been stolen outside of the graveyard in Bray while she was inside praying at the grave of her tragically departed child. She was distraught as she talked about her 'Little Johnny' and the lovely boy he was and the grief she was going through. And to think that while she was in crying at his graveside, some heartless, terrible person had stolen her car. The claims handler who took her call was actually very upset listening to the details.

But the red flags went up straightaway because claims made on policies that are less than three months old are always scrutinised; and because Ms McDonagh had also been a party to a previous recent claim. I started making phone calls. Bray garda station told me the car had been reported stolen alright but a check on their computer system also revealed that the same car had been crashed in Longford a few months previously. Longford garda station told me the car had been crashed and written off. It had been involved in a high-speed chase with a Garda patrol car and crashed into a wall after losing control and doing a couple of somersaults. The driver and passenger were also members of the travelling community, apparently related to Ms McDonagh. They were arrested and charged with dangerous driving as well as the theft of valuable goods which were recovered from the boot of the Primera. The car was subsequently towed out of Longford garda station on a trailer, never to be put back on the road again.

But the logbook and car keys somehow ended up in the possession of Ms McDonagh. We know this because she produced them when we invited her in for an interview about her claim. It seemed however that she'd never actually set eyes on the car itself. She wasn't even able to tell us the colour of it, even though it would have been in the logbook, or how many doors it had, or anything about its interior. I remember asking her if it had a sunroof or not and she wasn't able to tell me. She lost her cool fairly quickly and accused us of trying to bully her and stormed out of the building.

Part of my job was to assess bogus claims to see if they contained enough evidence of criminal fraud to refer them to the Gardaí for investigation. In this case there was more than enough evidence of premeditated criminal behaviour. We referred it to the Gardaí and she was duly prosecuted. It subsequently transpired that she wasn't married, didn't have any kids and therefore didn't have a darling child buried in Bray graveyard. She pleaded guilty in court and the judge gave her a suspended sentence. Judges often had a habit of treating offences differently if the defendant was caught before he or she had received the ill-gotten money. Same with robberies and the like. If the culprit was intercepted during the act or before it, they often got off with a lighter sentence.

The woman in this case had moved up in cars from a rust bucket, a ten-year old Micra or whatever, to a brand-new Primera and this became another red flag under the new regime at AXA: any customer who was suddenly moving up from a banger to a new car or a much more expensive model should be checked out. That became company policy and within weeks of this episode, another traveller lady came into our office in Bantry looking for insurance on a year-old car having previously been insured for something that was almost worthless. The manager in Bantry, as in every office, had been alerted by our SIU to be on the lookout for exactly this kind of scenario. So he asked her to call back with the new car so he could see it for himself. She promised she would but never did; almost certainly it was another scam averted.

Claims for compensation from Travellers were consistently disproportionate in number to the population of the travelling community. I think all insurance companies had similar statistics. It was just a regular feature of my experience in AXA.

Personal injuries were a common claim among the population in general, including the dreaded whiplash. There was a building contractor from Dublin who had a collision on a narrow road in Wexford with a local farmer. The contractor's son was in the passenger seat. The guards were called, the drivers were breathalysed, and it turned out the local farmer was over the limit and duly prosecuted for drunk driving. Seemingly encouraged by this development, the contractor and his son submitted claims to us for personal injuries. They produced medical records to show they'd suffered whiplash and that their respective backs had been significantly damaged as a result. The perennial problem with whiplash is that it does exist as a condition, but it doesn't show up in x-rays or scans. It's not like a broken leg. It is very hard to establish definitive medical proof of it in a patient. That's why it can be used as a sort of catch-all condition for insurees submitting personal injury claims.

We decided to investigate the claim. We hired a private investigator (PI) to monitor the pair of buckos. One day he saw them loading their golf bags into the boot of their car so naturally enough this aroused his suspicions. He tailed them to Castleknock Golf Club and had his video camera at the ready too. They parked up, the young fella got out and ran down to where the golf buggies were and he seemed very free in his movements. The two of them threw their bags into the back of the buggy and made their way to the first tee. There they did a series of stretching exercises which again seemed to show no sign of physical inhibition in their backs. When it came to striking the ball, there was nothing wrong with their golf swings either, at least not from a physical point of view. If they were having trouble with whiplash, there was no sign of it here. Our PI captured all this on camera before he was spotted lurking in the bushes by a golf ranger and ordered off the property. But he had all the evidence we needed. On top of that, we subpoenaed the golf club to get the respective handicaps of the father and son. Lo and behold, both their handicaps had gone down during the time the case was pending! We were able to get a register of all the times they'd played at the club during the same period of time. We presented to their legal team the video evidence and the records of their handicaps plus the list of dates on which they'd played full rounds of golf. After that, they were easy talked to; the claims died a death then and there.

At that time the insurance industry was trying to highlight the epidemic of bogus claims and I was roped in a few times to publicise the issue too. Which is how I ended up talking about it to Mary Kennedy and Marty Whelan one afternoon on their RTÉ show, *Open House*. Before he got into radio and television, Marty had worked with PMPA for five years selling insurance, so he had an interest in the subject too. Anyway, to showcase the problem for a TV audience, I brought in the footage of the Castleknock Arnold Palmer and son, flaking away at golf balls while pretending to us that they had severely damaged backs. RTÉ took the precaution of blacking out their faces for fear of legal trouble, but the pair went ahead and threatened to sue the makers of *Open House* anyway. Tyrone Productions were the company in question and they went into a panic when they got the threatening legal correspondence. But I told them there wasn't a hope in hell that the duo would go through with it and that's how it turned out.

Then there was the case of the Harley Davidson and its Polish owner who had a lucky escape, apparently, when he came off the bike at a T-junction at the back of the Carton House estate outside of Leixlip. He allegedly swerved to avoid hitting another car and the bike ended up crashing into a wall and being badly damaged. The car had two other Eastern Europeans in it and they gave evidence to the guards that they'd come around the road too wide and the motorcyclist had to take evasive action to avoid them. Fortunately, he didn't suffer any personal injuries himself. But the bike was so badly damaged that he claimed for its full value against the comprehensive policy he'd taken out with AXA. Now, we weren't talking about a Honda 50 here. A Harley Davidson was much more expensive than a lot of cars. Our friend had an Irish logbook and registration number for it, having imported it himself from America. We knew that the circumstances of the accident in Leixlip sounded suspicious, but, overall, his story seemed too watertight to challenge. But we had a salvage dealer in Enniscorthy and when he took the bike away and started examining it, his suspicions were aroused too. He inputted the chassis number into an online search and the same model showed up as having been for sale in Baton Rouge, Louisiana. But the vendor in Baton Rouge was getting rid of it for one good reason: it had been badly damaged. There were photographs of the crashed bike in the advert and they were showing the exact same damage as the bike that hit the wall in Leixlip. It was the same machine: same colour, same make, same chassis number. Basically, the owner had bought it from the vendor in Baton Rouge, presumably for small money, imported it, insured it with AXA as a perfectly good Harley Davidson and proceeded to stage the accident. We brought him in for interview; he stuck to his story but we point-blank refused to pay out. In fact, I reported it to the Gardaí as a clear-cut fraud case and they duly followed up on it, but the investigation ran into the sand when they decided in headquarters not to spend the money on sending a detective to Louisiana. To make the case stand up in court, a detective would have to interview the vendor in Baton Rouge to confirm all the relevant details regarding the Harley and its sale and shipping to the buyer in Ireland. They refused to authorise the trip and the investigation ground to a halt. I'd imagine our Polish friend was relieved about that, albeit that he'd lost a fair amount of money on his venture overall.

One of the things that most of these chancers had in common was a seemingly very naive idea about insurance companies and how they operate. In fact, I often wondered if they thought we were stupid or something. They seemed to think that people who worked in insurance were fairly gullible and that they, on the other hand, were very smart, and that they'd be able to pull a fast one and get away with it no bother at all. How ignorant could you be? Insurance companies have been around for hundreds of years and they haven't made fortunes by being gullible or loose with their money. It's quite the opposite in fact: you mess with them at your peril. They are formidably powerful institutions.

There was a chap from Nigeria who took the biscuit when it came to chancing one's arm. This fella, by the name of Chukwudi Ndu, was living in Dublin and submitted a claim for €16,000 after his house was allegedly robbed in 2002. We never established if the robbery was for real or if it had been set up by himself and a few other cronies. But he submitted his claim for loss of possessions, including €10,000-worth of designer suits. Now you wouldn't have to be a very bright claims handler to take a second look at this kind of an effort. Ten thousand euro for designer suits? Naturally enough, we invited him into our offices to discuss the matter. He obviously anticipated this move so on the day, he was able to produce a raft of receipts from various clothes outlets in Nigeria. We proceeded to drill down into the details about the robbery, what he was doing with all these suits, the naira currency and its conversion rate into euro, etc. He got very aggressive and angry with us, throwing his hands up and raising his voice and shouting that he couldn't understand our accents and what we were saying. Quite frankly, he was an awful bollocks. We refused to pay and he decided to take us to court for the money. It dragged on for years, even though we contacted a loss adjuster in Nigeria who conducted an investigation on the ground and came back to us with a fairly succinct report: the shops named in the receipts produced by Ndu didn't exist. We told his legal representative all this, but our hero insisted on continuing with the legal action. Eventually in May 2008 the case was due to be heard in court. We flew in the loss adjuster from Nigeria at a cost of €3,000, and had our witnesses and evidence and legal representatives assembled and ready to go, all done at a lot of cost too. It was only then, at the eleventh hour, that Ndu decided to drop the case and walk away. He definitely should have been prosecuted for fraud, but it didn't happen for one reason or another.

If it's one thing for complete outsiders to think they can pick up handy money, it's another thing altogether for insiders to try their luck. We're talking about internal fraud here, employees within the insurance industry who know very well what they are taking on. But I suppose this is the very thing that tempts them – their insider knowledge. They know the system, they practise the procedures every day, they see the money coming in and they see the money going out. So they can identify what they think are weak links in the chain and I guess a few of them are tempted to exploit the loophole and divert a little of the cash flow their way. There was one major case of internal fraud in AXA during my ten years there.

Danny O'Halloran had skimmed off €1.6 million before he was caught. He had spent his working life with AXA so he knew the system upside down. He was in his mid-forties when he decided to go over to the dark side. It wasn't so much that a weakness in the system fell into his lap and he couldn't resist the temptation, it was a calculated and opportunist crime that he perpetrated repeatedly for nearly five years.

O'Halloran was a claims handler and it was in this role that he began siphoning off money. Basically, he would re-open insurance claims that had been settled. The first step was to change the name of the genuine claimant to another name. Let's say Mrs Murphy had been paid €5,000 for genuine damages to her house or car or whatever. He would open Mrs Murphy's file on the computer and change the name and address. The next step was to wait until a colleague had left their computer terminal open; using their ID he would open up the file he'd just tampered with and authorise a cheque for payment of that claim. The next step was to pounce on the cheque after it was issued but before it left the building. He knew the system so well he was able to track each stage of the process. The cheques would be brought down to the post room for mailing from there. He was on first name terms with the staff there so he'd just saunter in and ask them to find the relevant envelope because, he'd explain, this person would be calling into the office to collect it and he would hand it over to them. The final step was to take these cheques and lodge them into a bank account he operated in his wife's maiden name, or another account belonging to a friend, an alcoholic who was living in a one-room flat on the Cabra Road. He had authorised access to these accounts. In fact, he had ATM cards for them. Again, this raised the old problem of banks not doing enough due diligence on accounts showing unusual amounts of transactions or unexplained revenue streams.

O'Halloran engineered these scams on average three or four times a month for the guts of five years. Each of them was below the value of €6,300 because claims handlers didn't have authorisation to approve valuations above that amount. But he was defrauding about €20,000 a month on average.

Eventually there was a glitch in the process that one day led to the whole thing unravelling in the summer of 2004. I came into the office one Monday morning having been away on holidays and John O'Neill summoned me straight to his office. 'We have a problem,' he said. They'd rumbled the scam and while they were investigating, O'Halloran had gone off on sick leave. He'd held his hands up straightaway and confessed everything. But he told one of the supervisors that he wanted to deal with me only. I'd gotten on well with him; in fact, he used to confide in me and ask me for advice. Everyone got a shock, myself included. Danny was a nice fella and a trusted employee. He'd been there a long time and nobody ever dreamed he'd be capable of doing something like this. He was always coming back from the bakery around the corner with cakes and buns and scones and the like. It turned out that he was often coming back laden with goodies when he'd just lodged another five or six grand to one of his bank accounts.

We arranged to meet outside Glasnevin Cemetery; that was the meeting spot he chose. I could see he was a broken man. He told me the whole story and said he wanted to admit his guilt to the whole fraud. I tried to be as sympathetic with him as I could be but obviously had to tell him that we'd be referring it to the Gardaí for criminal investigation. He nodded his head; he knew it was unavoidable and said he would fully co-operate with the guards. It became a large and lengthy investigation, led by Declan Daly, then a very experienced detective sergeant, now a detective chief superintendent. O'Halloran was duly charged and remanded on bail. I subsequently bumped into him down in the Four Courts one day during one of the remand hearings and he blanked me completely. Didn't want to talk to me; didn't want anything to do with me.

It came before the courts in July 2006; he was fifty-two at that stage. He pleaded guilty to twenty-five sample charges from a total of 178 counts on the indictment of defrauding AXA Insurance on multiple dates between 1999 and 2004 to the value of €1.1 million. The full extent of the fraud hadn't emerged at this stage. His barrister told Judge Frank O'Donnell at the Dublin Circuit Criminal Court that O'Halloran had the means to pay back €600,000. He would forfeit his pension and shares in the company and he would sell two properties he owned in Co. Kerry. I actually flew down to Farranfore twice to view the houses and meet with local auctioneers to get them valued and sold. I think this was why he turned totally cold on me that day in the Four Courts. He'd obviously heard I'd been down in Kerry looking to get the houses off him and he'd been hoping to hold onto them.

The court also heard that he'd only €12,000 left in his accounts. Some of it was spent on home improvements at his house in Finglas, and on doing up the properties in

Kerry, but according to his lawyer, Conor Devally, most of it had been 'frittered away'. He had been very generous with cash gifts to relatives and extended family and to other people that found themselves in financial difficulty. Devally said O'Halloran had been working in AXA for thirty-one years and couldn't provide any reason for why he did what he did. He was a man with poor self-esteem, a reformed alcoholic who liked to shower those around him with generosity 'in a bizarre way to pay for their good will'. He said that his client 'went to great pains' to emphasise that neither his wife nor the other friend had anything to do with the fraudulent activity. As for the shortfall that would still exist after he'd returned €600,000, Devally said that O'Halloran was now driving a taxi and working 'all the hours God gave' to raise funds not only to pay the money back but to provide a secure future for his wife and nine-year-old daughter. His taxi was not insured by AXA.

Judge O'Donnell said it was a really sad case. 'If I had only Mr O'Halloran and his family to think about it would be handy, but this is an extremely serious crime and there is no way I can gloss over that. Irrespective of our individual opinions of banks and financial institutions, when they are undermined it undermines our society.' He revoked O'Halloran's bail and remanded him in custody for sentencing. The following November he sentenced him to three years in prison, the last two suspended. The Judge said it was 'a personal but self-inflicted tragedy' and that his wife and young child were innocent victims.

O'Halloran was released in 2007 having spent less than a year in jail. But after all the sob stories and the talk of making good on the money and working night and day to pay it back, AXA had to return to court in April 2008 to get a judgment against him – he had only paid back €30,000 by then. The €600,000 promised in court in 2006 hadn't materialised. And it was during the proceedings in 2008 that the full extent of the fraud was revealed. A report in the *Irish Independent* quoted John O'Neill as saying that O'Halloran had in fact stolen €1.6 million, not €1.1m. 'We have a duty on behalf of our honest policy holders to pursue fraudsters to the full extent of the law,' he said. 'At the end of the day this money is our customers' money and is reflected in the premiums that we charge.' The High Court granted AXA the €1.6 million judgment. 'What we want to know,' added John, 'is where is all the money gone?'

O'Halloran's solicitor argued that his client had signed over his €400,000 pension to AXA and had agreed to the sale of his house in Finglas and his properties in Kerry. But AXA had encountered legal difficulties when they tried to cash in the pension. And the sale of the two houses in Kerry, valued at about €250,000 each, was also legally complicated because his wife was a joint owner and claimed entitlement to half the proceeds.

In May 2008 the matter came before the Taxing Master as AXA tried to enforce the High Court judgment. Once again, we tried to get the question answered: where had all the money gone? O'Halloran came under sustained pressure to explain. According to an *Irish Independent* report:

> He initially said he had spent the money on his 'lifestyle' but later acknowledged that he

had only a 'normal amount' of suits and shoes, leading to the conclusion that the money had not been spent on clothing. He added that he had bought his wife 'some jewellery' and had 'taken taxis and an occasional flight to Kerry'. Mr O'Halloran then volunteered that he had 'bought a treehouse'. After almost two hours of exchanges, the Taxing Master adjourned the case until June 4.

The business of getting the money back dragged on for years. 'We had a similar case in the UK,' said John O'Neill at the time, 'it only took a few months to get the case through the courts, the person got several years in jail and repaid most of the money. In Ireland it takes years to get to court, the sentences are very short and the money doesn't get paid back.'

He was spot on about that.

I must say, I thoroughly enjoyed my ten-plus years working with AXA Insurance. The integration into the private sector was seamless and I was accepted into their fold with total respect. I sometimes believed I was adopting the role of agony aunt/uncle as whenever anyone in the company had a problem, either themselves or a family member, the one pathway was straight to my desk. I never turned anyone away and assisted them in whatever way I could. That was not part of my contract, but assisting people came as second nature to me, continuing my life in law enforcement where common sense played a large part of my lifetime and is still playing a part to this day.

21

IN SICKNESS AND IN HEALTH

The undercurrent was dragging me out and I was fighting to swim back in to shore. But I couldn't beat the undertow. I was thrashing away but I was losing my strength and I wasn't a strong swimmer anyway. I was starting to panic in the water.

We were on holidays in Benalmadena on the Costa del Sol, myself and Elizabeth and Ann and Paddy. Ann is Elizabeth's sister. It was May 2015. We were down at the beach every day. This particular afternoon I threw myself into the water as usual. There was a lovely big wave coming in and of course I went out like a bold boy and dived into the wave. After a few seconds I turned around to swim back but, all of a sudden, I was getting nowhere. Even though the waves were coming into shore I was being dragged out by this powerful undercurrent.

I called for help but not very loudly because I wasn't far out and I didn't want to be heard shouting for help. Paddy, Ann's husband, heard me shouting alright and the three of them on the beach were looking at me, but they saw me splashing away and thought I was there enjoying myself! I was far from enjoying myself. I tried to go underwater but couldn't make any progress, I flipped onto my back and tried the backstroke, but that wasn't working either. Eventually I made headway through a final burst of ignorance and adrenaline and got in as far as the shallow water. But when I tried to stand up, my legs wouldn't hold me. These little waves were actually knocking me over. Paddy then spotted me struggling and came out and had to assist me back to the beach. I was weak as a kitten by now; I was shivering and shaking with panic too; I was in an awful state.

We made our way back to the hotel and Elizabeth called a doctor from reception. The doctor came and checked me and put a stethoscope on me. He knew straightaway that something was wrong and called an ambulance. My heart had an irregular beat, so he gave me an injection to stabilise it. I was loaded into the ambulance outside the hotel. In the local hospital they discovered my heartbeat was so irregular they decided to give it an electric shock. I had two tracks on my chest from the shock treatment, as if a hot iron had been put down on it. But it brought my heartbeat back to normal. I was put on medication and stayed the night in hospital.

That day in the sea in Benalmadena was probably the beginning of the end of the good health I'd enjoyed all my life. The sheer panic in the water had caused my heart to start pounding out of its chest and triggered the irregular heartbeat. I was diagnosed with atrial fibrillation.

The following November I had a stroke. I was sixty-eight. It happened on a Sunday morning. The day before, the family had been at the christening in Leixlip Church of baby Seán Grealis, our ninth grandchild. From there we adjourned to a pub/restaurant in Maynooth for the celebrations. I was in great form. In fact, I probably drank not wisely but too well! I knocked back a fair few pints of Guinness and when I had my fill of stout, I promoted myself to the top shelf and made short work of a few very nice Black Bush whiskeys.

So, when I woke up the next morning with a pain in my head, I put it down to the excesses of the night before. I got out of bed, went downstairs, came back upstairs into our bedroom and promptly collapsed on the bed. Elizabeth was in bed and knew immediately that something was wrong. She rang 999 and the operator started talking her through a few protocols. I was only told all of this afterwards. I don't remember any of it. The operator asked Elizabeth if I could lift my arms. She lifted my right arm and it was fine. But when she tried to lift my left arm, nothing happened. It wasn't moving. The operator said it sounded like a stroke; she said there was an ambulance on its way. Apparently I protested, saying I didn't want an ambulance pulling up outside our house. Anyway, it duly arrived and the two fellas came up the stairs with a wheelchair, lifted me into it and carried me down and into the van. And that was fair going for them, given I weighed about sixteen and a half stone.

I got sick in the ambulance en route to the Mater. I remember apologising to the medics and they saying not to worry about it. In the Mater they did an MRI scan which showed a clot on the brain. I was transferred from there to Beaumont Hospital where a surgeon was available to perform a thrombectomy – a procedure whereby the clot is removed from the brain. Time is of the essence in stroke situations. I was lucky that it happened to me at home and not when I was out somewhere on my own. Thankfully every step of this emergency, from the 999 call to the ambulance, the Mater and Beaumont, all went smoothly and efficiently. I was a very lucky man. Other poor unfortunates aren't so lucky.

From Beaumont I was taken back to the Mater and placed in the high dependency ward on my own. Elizabeth and our sons David and Brendan were waiting for me there. I was conscious; I had my senses about me, if not my wits. My phone rang later that evening. Elizabeth answered it. It was Padraig Melvin, secretary of the Mayo Golf Society in Dublin. Padraig sadly went to his eternal reward in March 2021. I was a member of the golf society and we were due to have a meeting the next day. So I took the phone and explained to Padraig where I was and why I was there. And says I, 'Sure, we can have the meeting in the ward here. The lads can come in and we'll hold the meeting here in the Mater hospital.' Maybe the effect of the Black Bush the night before still hadn't worn off! Needless to say, that idea was quickly abandoned.

I was transferred to the acute stroke ward the next day. I woke up from a nap to find a priest standing over me. I immediately assumed he was the hospital chaplain and says I to him, 'You're a ringer for our parish priest in Leixlip, Fr McNamara.'

'That's just as well,' he replied, 'because I am the parish

priest in Leixlip!' Fr John told me he'd met Elizabeth at Mass that morning and she'd asked him to pray for me, and fair play to him he went one step further and came in himself to talk to me in person.

I spent two weeks convalescing in the Mater before being transferred to Connolly Hospital, Blanchardstown, for two more weeks to take the first steps of what would be a long rehabilitation. My left arm and hand needed a lot of work to start functioning again. My left leg was damaged too although I could hobble along on it; I didn't need crutches. It's the nerve endings that are affected, like in your fingertips and in your jaw and your leg. Rehab is all about exercising them every day to try and get them working again. They sent me out to the hospital in Clane first to get assessed by the therapists there. Luckily, I was able to talk and read the newspaper and communicate more or less fine so they decided I didn't need speech and language therapy. Instead, I would need occupational therapy and of course physiotherapy.

My rehab programme would be conducted as an outpatient in the old Baggot Street Hospital. I would go in there one day a week for a couple of hours where the staff would work on me and give me a set of exercises to do daily when I got home. I did those exercises religiously every single day. I was absolutely determined to get back to my old self in every way. I knew how lucky I was even to be offered a shot at a full recovery. I had been reached in time; they had got to me early enough to minimise the damage. I'd been saved by the bell. And I considered myself too fit and too young to be going around disabled in any way. The rehab process would be tedious and frustrating at times, but once I felt the first signs of progress, I kept going and gradually started getting stronger.

It was not all plain sailing. A basic thing like using a knife and fork became very frustrating. Something I had done all my life, I couldn't do. Obviously, you'd have the knife in your right hand and that was fine, but I couldn't hold the fork in my left. You'd be trying to co-ordinate something that came naturally and you couldn't do it. That was strange and vexatious. My left leg, I'd be dragging it along with me and getting frustrated and annoyed when it wouldn't work. From time to time my annoyance would get the better of me and on a few occasions, I took it out on poor Elizabeth. We'd been married forty-two years at that stage and we'd got on so well. I never raised my voice to her in my life and suddenly now I was erupting into outbursts. It was totally wrong on my part and I feel remorseful about it. I was struggling to cope with my new reality and mentally it put me on edge. But she looked after me through thick and thin and honestly, I'd have been lost without her love and support at a time when I was at my most vulnerable.

* * *

I had first set eyes on Elizabeth Cooney at a dance in the National Ballroom on 23 May 1971. It was a Wednesday night. Unfortunately, neither of us can remember what band was playing that night. But I do remember leaving her home to her digs in Innisfallen Parade on the North

Circular Road and getting her phone number. And I also remember vividly going home to the flat on Harcourt Street I shared with a few other Garda colleagues and waking up Pat Morgan to make an announcement. 'Pat,' says I, 'I met the mother of my children tonight.' I was smitten. We just clicked. I thought she was gorgeous; she had a lovely figure and we jived all night. I was no good at waltzing. As a full forward I'd waltzed through a few defences in my time, but when it came to waltzing on the dance floor, I was tripping over myself.

I wore a blue blazer and white polo neck that night in the National. The following weekend was the Whit bank holiday and I was off to London to play for Mayo in the annual GAA tournament at Wembley stadium. At the time it was a real prestige event. They were exhibition games in hurling and football. That year, Cork played Tipp in the hurling while Kerry played Meath and we played Derry in two football semi-finals. The matches were televised and I was interviewed at half-time in the hurling match. Meanwhile, Elizabeth had gone home to Moneygall for the weekend. Sitting on the Tipperary–Offaly border, the Cooneys were on the Tipperary side of Moneygall. Anyway, they were watching the games at home on a black-and-white telly when next thing I appear on the screen, being interviewed – and wearing the same blue blazer and white polo neck I had on me in the National a few days earlier. Elizabeth recognises me straightaway. 'That's the fella who brought me home from the dance last Wednesday!' says she. And she ran out to the garden where her father was doing a bit of work to bring him in and show him the fella she met at the dance. I had never told her I was going away to play Gaelic in Wembley or that I was a footballer at all.

The following week I gave her a call as promised and we met up and we started going steady. Elizabeth was working as a legal secretary with a law firm in Foster Place. We began to make plans for our future and in September 1973 we were married. Séamus Ó Riain, GAA president between 1967 and 1970, was also from Moneygall and married to an aunt of Elizabeth. It was through his connection that Seán Ó Síocháin, the GAA's director general, ended up calling into our wedding reception in the Ormond Hotel in Nenagh. Bride and groom had a photo taken with Mr Ó Síocháin which ended up in one of the national newspapers the next day.

Our first child David came along in August 1974 followed by Sandra in '76, Brendan in '78 and Ailish in 1980. We moved from our first house in Palmerstown to our permanent home in Leixlip the same year. Elizabeth gave up her job after David was born to become a full-time mother and homemaker. I have to confess that I wasn't much use on the domestic front. I was a traditional Irish male of my time and place. I was focused on work and career while Elizabeth kept the home fires burning. In fact, I have to admit that I never changed a nappy in my life. I never did any ironing or really any kind of housework. Elizabeth was a fantastic mother and cook and homemaker and took care of all that. I know, I got away with murder! I see my sons and sons-in-law changing nappies and ironing clothes and doing the dishes and cooking food and of course, it's right and proper.

In all honesty I'm probably a more attentive grandfather than I was a father. I'd often see ould fellas out
wheeling prams and I'd stop and ask them did they ever
wheel their own children out in a pram and it'd be 'No, no
way!' They'd wheel their grandkids out alright but didn't
do it with their own kids. I was the same. I dunno, maybe
we thought we were too macho to be doing things like
that. Anyway, when the grandkids started coming along, I
was absolutely besotted with each and every one of them.
I have the time in retirement to enjoy them and I must say,
I'm stone mad about them. I couldn't live without them.

Gráinne, David's daughter, was the first of them and
she is very dear to us. She was very ill when she was born,
in October 2002, and had to go through an awful lot of
medical treatment in those early years. Elizabeth had been
dealing with breast cancer for a couple of years by then.
It was a terrible rough time for her and for us. Eventually
she made a full recovery and she was convinced that God
spared her in order to be able to look after wee Gráinne.
Happily everything worked out well in the end and
Gráinne has just sat her Leaving Cert and will hopefully
follow a career in paediatric nursing.

David followed in his old man's footsteps and joined
the Gardaí. I think he was always destined to follow me
in blue seeing as how he arrested the milkman when he
was only six years old. The milkman had come round to
collect his weekly payment and David met him at the front
door with a pair of my handcuffs. 'You're under arrest!'
he declared. The milkman played along with him and held
out his two arms to be handcuffed. David slapped the

cuffs on him and there was great hilarity, until it dawned on everyone that I had the keys of the cuffs with me at work! Panic ensued. Elizabeth rang me in a tizzy and I had to make an emergency dash from Dublin Castle to Palmerstown to free the poor man. When I got home, he was drinking tea in the kitchen holding the cup with both hands. In fairness, he saw the funny side of it and a great laugh was had by all.

Brendan became a carpenter and when I think of him as a child, it often puts me in mind of a late, great friend of mine, John Mulroy. John was from Mayo and had worked for twenty-five years with Pan American airlines, starting out as a clerk and working his way up to become director of communications. In the mid-1980s he joined the Associated Press news agency as director of international communications. John, his son Seán and Seán's wife Ingrid were on the Pan Am flight that was bombed and blown up over Lockerbie, Scotland, on 21 December 1988. The Mulroy family lost six loved ones in that terrorist atrocity. John's sister Bridget Concannon, her husband Thomas and their son Seán were also on the plane. They were planning to spend Christmas together in New York. A total of 270 people were murdered in the attack that day. It was the most tremendous shock to us all. And as it happened, the day before, a lovely parcel was delivered to our home from America. It was a Christmas present from John to our children: three beautiful tracksuits embroidered with the names David, Sandra and Ailish. John had inadvertently forgotten about Brendan. And poor Brendan naturally enough was awful disappointed about being left out!

Then the devastating news about Lockerbie came through the following day. We were distraught of course. Then Brendan in his sadness and innocence remarked, 'I'll never get one now from poor John.'

Brendan and Sarah have three kids: Sonny, Penny Mae and, last but most certainly not least, Myles William, born in February 2021, our eleventh grandchild. David and Sharon had a boy together, James, our third grandchild. Sandra and Ailish, as it turned out, married two men from Mulranny who are also in the guards. As a family we'd been going on holidays to my home place since they were nippers and they loved it so much that the girls ended up finding their husbands there! Sandra and Bobby have two boys, Seán and Mark Grealis. Ailish and Colm have Padraig, Cillian, Caoimhe and Darragh Reilly.

Luckily enough, they reckon I'm the best granddad in the world! Relationships have changed dramatically since I was a young fella. I think kids nowadays have a tendency to dote on their grandparents, whereas in my day you were half afraid of them. My maternal grandfather was long dead before I was born and my maternal grandmother lived with us in Newport, but I was very young when she died. My father's father was a very serious, quiet kind of man. I never had a conversation with him really until right at the very end of his life. Peter McGee was living in Tuam at the time with his daughter, my aunt Aggie. I paid them a visit after playing for the Mayo under-21s against Galway in Tuam Stadium in 1968. He asked me if I scored. I told him I'd scored a couple of points and there wasn't much more said. I think he was proud of me playing for Mayo alright, but he wouldn't have been able to say as much. I headed back to Dublin that evening to resume my apprenticeship in Pearse Street and the following morning he was dead.

It's a totally different kind of relationship between children and grandparents nowadays. Like, they'll tell you to your face that they love you and they're mad for hugs and stories and spending time with you. The Covid-19 lockdowns in 2020 and 2021 have had a terrible effect on society in general, but it's been very hard on grandkids and grandparents too, not being able to see each other. I know it affected some of ours. Caoimhe and Cillian had to get cushions made with photos of myself and Elizabeth superimposed on them so they would be able to hug us and feel close to us in our absence. There's been a price to pay for all this bloody cocooning. Anyway, we've got our vaccines now and hopefully normal life will be resuming sooner rather than later.

**

The rehab from my stroke picked up pace in the years that followed. A constant consolation for me throughout the struggle was my religious faith. When I came out of hospital, I started going to 9.30 a.m. Mass every morning, in Leixlip. Now, they say that some people only start praying when they need something badly and I'd be guilty on all counts of that. It was my health crisis that sent me back to the Church in a serious way. I'd never left it really. I'd been an observant Catholic, but in my hour of need I turned to God and in particular to one of my favourite saints, Padre Pio. For some reason I felt I could talk to Padre Pio and I felt that he would hear me. It gave me strength for my recovery, believing I had this holy man by my side. You need someone there inside your brain to help you and I called on him many times and he answered my prayers. That in turn reinforced my faith further. For the last six years I find, if I'm in bed and can't sleep, I start praying and I drift off and wake up the following morning after a great night's sleep. I have read a lot about Saint Pio and it's one of my ambitions when the pandemic is over to make a pilgrimage to his home place in Italy.

But a policeman is never off duty, not even in the house of prayer. You'd think the house of God should be a no-go area for the wickedness of man, but sadly we know too well that it is not.

One Sunday evening many years ago, Elizabeth and I were at Mass in Leixlip. This was a few years before I retired from the police force. Out of the side of my eye I caught a glimpse of a man and woman coming down one of the aisles. I'd guess they were in their thirties. My professional curiosity was piqued. They looked unusual for Leixlip. They weren't regulars in the church; they were strangers as far as I could tell. Then I figured that we normally went to Sunday Mass in the morning, not evening, and maybe they were regulars at the evening service. But they caught my eye again at communion time. They went up to receive Holy Communion from the side where I was sitting but, unusually, didn't return to their seats. Instead, they went to the far transept beside the sacristy where they knelt down. After Mass I bumped into a young Garda based in Kevin Street who had also noticed this couple. And he noticed them for a reason: they were well-known criminals from the city centre; he had come across them before in the job.

We decided to go back in and have a word with the parish priest who was an elderly man then and has since passed on. Lo and behold, the priest told us that the couple had paid him a visit in the sacristy. The male had asked him to pray for an uncle of his who was dying. The priest was probably a bit innocent. He didn't notice anything untoward about them – apart from the fact that there was a strong smell of drink off the male. And where was the female, we asked, while the male was asking for prayers for his uncle? The priest only thought about it then. Come to think of it, he said, she had discreetly wandered off while he was listening to her partner's tale of woe about his uncle. In other words, she was casing the joint. The Sunday evening Mass was the last of five Masses over a normal weekend and the church collections would all be bundled together and kept in a safe in the sacristy overnight before being lodged in the bank on Monday. I immediately contacted Lucan garda station by phone and told them the story. (There was no garda station in Leixlip at the time.) I advised them to have personnel present at the church first thing Monday morning in case a robbery was about to be staged.

It didn't happen; the money was lodged as per usual. But I got back onto Lucan and told them to have a few detectives on duty at the church the following Sunday evening. It looked to me like this had been a dry run for a planned robbery. Seven days later I was back in the church, this time less as a communicant and more as a policeman. The same couple did not reappear. But another couple did, two males, who again looked out of place. They positioned themselves in the transept beside the sacristy door just as the previous duo had done. As soon as Mass was over, they made for the sacristy. And I made for the sacristy too. There was no sign of the detectives from Lucan. Inside, one of the men was engaging the priest in conversation while the other fella was snooping around the back. I went and confronted this fella. I asked him if I could help him with anything. He said no, he was fine, he was just killing time while his friend was talking to the priest. But he looked rattled. We rejoined the priest and the other fella. I asked the pair of them where they were from. They were on edge now, the two of them, so I told them I was a Garda superintendent and I wanted to know what they were doing here. The first fella bolted for the door straightaway. I grabbed the second fella and we started grappling and struggling. He got very angry and very aggressive. He produced a needle from a jacket pocket and told me he was HIV positive and that he'd stab me with it. At this stage I reckoned discretion would be the better part of valour. In my experience, if someone wants to get away from you badly enough, they'll get away, no matter how hard you try to hold him. There's a desperation to the way they fight and struggle. It is very hard to keep someone at bay on your own for longer than a few minutes. It's amazing the strength they will muster out of sheer panic and desperation. So I let him go and off he took like a scalded cat. The elderly priest was looking at all this in a state of confusion. The penny still hadn't dropped with him. He had no idea how serious the situation could have been. He had a better idea when we found a length of rope on the floor that the second fella had dropped, or that had fallen out of his pocket during the struggle. It was the rope that they were going to use to tie up the priest.

About five minutes later the detectives arrived from Lucan. They were too late. I was very annoyed by that. They hadn't done their job properly. Out in the car park, the two criminals had abandoned the car they arrived in. We found more rope in it. There had been a spate of church robberies in the region that involved priests being tied up and the sacristies being raided. Through the car we were able to link a connection to the culprits, who were subsequently arrested and charged with a string of other robberies in Kildare. But thankfully they were stopped in time from adding Leixlip church to their list of crimes and I took great satisfaction from my role in being able to foil them.

During lockdown, Leixlip church was out of bounds, like every other house of worship in the country. Thankfully through the miracle of the Internet I was able to get Mass online any day of the week I wanted. My first port of call, as it were, was my old home church in Newport. I would log onto their Facebook page most mornings and partake in the service remotely. It was the best that could be done in the circumstances. In Castleisland in Co. Kerry, Fr Mossy Brick does a dedicated service to Padre Pio once a month which includes a Mass and rosary and I would tune into that also.

Before Covid-19 turned our world upside down in the spring of 2020, I was going great guns in my recovery from the stroke. I was back on the golf course, I was swimming in the pool and working out in the gym in Maynooth and I was out walking practically every day. For two years I visited the rehab centre in Baggot Street every week where the brilliant staff took care of me and supervised my recovery. Aisling was my occupational therapist, Sarah was my physiotherapist, and they were absolutely wonderful to me. I couldn't have made the recovery I did without them; they will have my deepest gratitude always.

One day Sarah did the grip test to see how my left hand was recovering. It turned out to be stronger than my right hand. That was the day they said to me they didn't need to see me back in the place. I was well on the road. They were delighted with my progress.

Then I suffered a setback in March 2019 when I took a fall in Drumcondra train station. I had taken the train in from Leixlip to watch Mayo play Kerry in the national league final. I was coming down the steps and missed the last step and down I went. I got up and dusted myself off and walked down to Croke Park and back to the station after the game. But a few days later my knee swelled up. An old cartilage injury that had been operated on fifty years earlier came back to haunt me. I had keyhole surgery on it in September 2019 but unfortunately it never came right; it's still stiff and sore and I can't bend it. I have to use a buggy on the golf course and it has curtailed my long walks.

The twelve months and more spent cocooning hasn't helped my fitness programme, but I was in great shape physically before the pandemic took over and I fully intend to get back to it as soon as society starts opening up again.

In the years immediately after my illness, I started going to Croke Park for reasons other than football. The Irish Heart Foundation organised a series of annual conferences there for stroke survivors and I attended them for three years running. I found the lectures and talks given by various medical experts very interesting and helpful. The Irish Heart Foundation does brilliant work in promoting awareness around strokes and they've published a variety of excellent booklets on every aspect of sickness involving the heart.

EPILOGUE

As I write these final few words in early 2022, I am bearing down on my seventy-fifth birthday. Naturally it is an ancient age to my grandkids, but to me it doesn't seem ancient at all. I don't feel it anyway, despite the trials and tribulations of the last few years. I thank God for the years He has given me and I'm praying that He gives me many more.

It has been a wonderful life. I have been blessed in so many ways and I hope I made some sort of contribution to our society through the work I did. Looking back on it now, I can appreciate better how interesting and stimulating it was. You came across all sorts of people, some who lived lives I could never have imagined growing up in the innocence of a Newport childhood. It was a working life spent in the shadow of fraud. A generation of police officers have been fighting that good fight since I retired. It's a battle that will never end. I am glad that I played my part.

I am glad that I played my part for Mayo too! I will be supporting our footballers for as long as there's breath in my body, just as I will always be supporting the Garda Síochána. They serve our country well. It is a police force